Foreword

MESSAGE OF INTRODUCTION FROM BRIAN CULLEN, CHAIRMAN, FOYNES FLYING BOAT MUSEUM.

D0885242

"Tempus fugit"

It really is hard to believe that the Museum is now in it's twentieth year.

What started off as a small venue commemorating an important period and story in aviation history has grown beyond our wildest dreams.

Along the way we acquired ownership of the entire original terminal building. This paved the way to quadruple the exhibition area and cover-in the courtyard for multipurpose use and seating for over 300 people.

A very popular new children's section was added.

The world's only full size replica of a Boeing 314 flying boat was constructed to exacting detail and even some who worked as crew on board these majestic machines, and have come to visit it, marvel at the time warp experience.

Reconstruction of the original control tower, a very exciting development, was made possible through generous sponsorship from the Irish Aviation Authority for which we are very grateful.

Next phase when funds become available will be enlargement of the shop, reconstruction of the O'Regan restaurant and a new exhibition on maritime history of Foynes Port.

But perhaps the biggest success of all has been the joy of so many visitors from all corners of the world who have taken the trouble to write to us to tell of the pleasure their visit to the museum has given them. This has much to do with the unwavering enthusiasm and passion of our wonderful staff and board members many of whom have been part of the story from the very beginning all those years ago.

Brian Cullen

Chairman

FOYNES
FLYING BOAT
MUSEUM

CONTENTS

Left Above: Winch to pull B314s in by the tail.

Left: 6th August 1945, Pan Am Pacific Clipper, the first flying boat to use the new docking proceedure which took just 6 minutes—a considerable saving in time over the previous system of handling from the bouy. Coxswain Denis Herraghty, Chief Mechanic Al Stephan and Station Manager Harrold Egger discuss work with mechanics Ray Moore and Pete Wlydgka.

Introduction

Terminal Building and control tower.

FOYNES, COUNTY LIMERICK HAS BEEN AN IMPORTANT SEA PORT SINCE 1846, IT'S NATURAL HARBOUR, THIRTY MILES FROM THE ATLANTIC OCEAN AND 24 MILES FROM LIMERICK CITY, IS SHELTERED. BUT DURING THE LATE 1930S AND EARLY 1940S, THIS TRANQUIL TOWN ON THE SHANNON ESTUARY WAS TRANSFORMED INTO A MAJOR INTERNATIONAL AIR-BASE.

Foynes became a fulcrum point for traffic between the United States and Europe. Passengers travelling from, for example, New York to Lisbon, had to travel through Foynes. International businessmen, famous politicians, film stars, active-service men and refugees from the war in Europe travelling from anywhere in Europe to anywhere in the United States had to come to Foynes. For a few years, Foynes was the centre of the Aviation World.

The prime mover in the development of transatlantic air services was Pan American Airways. The company, under its dynamic President, Juan Trippe, employed Charles Lindbergh as a consultant to act as a pathfinder for their Pacific and Atlantic routes.

In 1933, Lindbergh arrived at Southampton and later made a survey flight to Ireland to examine possible sites for a proposed Flying Boat base. Having looked at Galway and Cork, he ultimately concentrated on the Rineanna Peninsula, on the County Clare shores of the River Shannon. The Irish government carried out many surveys of the peninsula, and the results were then communicated to the British Air Ministry and to Pan American.

In November 1935 at a conference in Ottawa, agreement was reached between the Governments of Britain, Canada, The Irish Free State, as it then was, and the Provincial Government of Newfoundland for the establishment of mail and passenger services across the North Atlantic. The original site on the Clare coast was not ready in time and an alternative had to be chosen.

It was also at this conference that Éamon de Valera included a vital clause "All aircraft on the transatlantic air service on the direct route shall stop at the Irish Free State Airport". This clause operated to the benefit of Shannon Airport until 1994 when the Irish Government changed the status of Shannon.

On Monday 16th December 1935 the Irish Times announced that Foynes in County Limerick had been chosen as the European Terminal for the proposed transatlantic air services.

The report certainly made the citizens of Cork sit up and take notice and the following Thursday a deputation from Cork visited Éamon de Valera in Dublin armed with considerable documentation to illustrate the outstanding position of Cork Harbour in relation to transatlantic and European traffic.

De Valera was not able to give the delegation any definite promises as he explained that the selection of the site was based primarily on technical considerations and was not a political decision.

On 19th October 1936 the Limerick Harbour Board were requested to attend a meeting in Dublin with the Minister for Industry and Commerce to discuss the project. The new airport, it was announced, was to be known as the Kilconry International Airport (a name which appears never to have been used) and its capital cost was reckoned to be not less than £500,000 and could possibly be much higher. It was to be located at Rineanna and if it was not ready in time for the first transatlantic services, the Port of Foynes, on the opposite bank of the Shannon would be used until the new airport was ready.

The quiet little village of Foynes, population of under 500 people, became the scene of feverish activity as radio equipment, radio operators and meteorologists arrived and set up their equipment.

The British Air Ministry assisted in the establishment of the forecasting service at Foynes. In 1936 Mr. Peters and two assistants moved over from Croyden installed themselves in a room at the Monteagle Arms Hotel—now the museum building—which had become the centre of operations at Foynes. In another room, radio equipment was installed and yet another part of the Hotel functioned as a control room.

However when the Irish Government approached the owners of the Monteagle Arms Hotel to discuss the purchase of the entire building, they were refused. So the Government took a compulsory purchase order on it—the first ever in Ireland. Similar preparations were underway at Botwood, Newfoundland and Shediac, New Brunswick. By the end of 1936 Foynes was now ready to receive the first experimental transatlantic flights.

Top: The Airport Hotel, built to accommodate the passengers of flying boats. Above: Main Street in Foynes.

THE PIONEERS

"IT'S IMPOSSIBLE." JUST AFTER WORLD WAR I, THIS WAS MOST PEOPLE'S REACTION TO BEING TOLD THAT SOME FOOLISH PILOT WAS GOING TO FLY ACROSS THE ATLANTIC. THE WEATHER WAS TREACHEROUS, YOU COULD ONLY NAVIGATE IF YOU COULD SEE THE SUN, MOON AND STARS, THERE WERE PRACTICALLY NO INSTRUMENTS AND NEWFOUNDLAND WAS 2,000 MILES FROM IRELAND. IT WAS IMPOSSIBLE—BUT THE NEWSPAPERS OFFERED CASH PRIZES, THE GOVERNMENTS OFFERED GLORY AND A LOT OF PEOPLE WERE GOING TO TRY.

Curtiss NC-4, sometime after the transatlantic test flight, 1919.

THE FIRST ACROSS THE ATLANTIC

The first aircraft to cross the Atlantic was the NC4 Flying Boat flown by Lieutenant Commander Read of the United States Navy in 1919.

On May 16th, three flying boats—NC1, NC3 and NC4, known as the "Nancies"—took off from Trepassy Bay, Newfoundland and flew into the Atlantic night. There were 68 destroyers marking the way with searchlights at intervals of fifty miles along the entire route. Five battleships—one every 400 miles acted as weather stations. The three flying boats were intended to cross the 2,000 miles of ocean using the ships as stepping stones.

By dawn the whole Atlantic was one gigantic cloud. Totally unforecast fog enveloped all three aircraft; heavy rain and high winds followed. Within minutes they were totally lost.

NC1 landed in mid-ocean to take stock of the situation; almost immediately the power part of her tail was swept away by the waves. After five hours of bailing water from the cockpit the crew were taken in tow by a Greek ship, the Ionia. But the line broke in the gale and NC1 became the first plane to go to the bottom of the Atlantic Ocean.

NC3 also decided to land. From 500 feet the sea didn't look too bad, but as the flying boat touched down she hit a huge swell, bounced back up into the air and then plunged into the water. Her hull was broken and her controls gone. They could hear the nearby destroyers on the radio, but they couldn't contact them. For two and a half days they taxied with a crew man hung on the tip of the starboard wing to keep the port wing out of the water. At Ponta Delgada in the Azores they lowered the distress signal, hoisted the stars and stripes and sailed stern first into the harbour.

NC4 followed all the ship stations until they ran into heavy fog and missed number 17. But at 09.30h the pilot peered through a gap in the cloud and saw a dark colour in the grey sea—the cliffs of the island of Flores. Fifteen hours and eighteen minutes after leaving Newfoundland, NC4 landed in the Azores.

On May 27th Lieutenant-Commander Read in the NC4 took off from Horta in the Azores and calmly crossed the bridge of warships to Portugal. Nine hours and 43 minutes later they landed at Lisbon. On May 30th, NC4 flew over the third and last 'boat bridge' from Lisbon to Plymouth in England. The Atlantic had been flown in a time of 53 hours and 58 minutes—spread over 23 days.

ALCOCK AND BROWN

On June 5th, 1919, John Alcock, Authur Whiten Brown and their two stuffed black cat mascots, Twinkletoes and Lucky Jim—landed their Vickers Vimy Bomber in a bog near Clifden, County Galway. They had become the first men to fly the Atlantic in one hop.

A crowd had gathered in Newfoundland the day before expecting to see them kill themselves, but at 16.28 GMT Brown, the navigator, tapped out on the wireless transmitter: "All well and started". It was the last message he sent. The tiny propeller that drove the transmitter then fell off.

Alcock flew on through the Atlantic mid-summer weather—fog, wind, hail, rain and snow—and just managed to pull out of a wild spin which left them pointing back to Newfoundland.

Brown later put into words the feelings of thousands who were to follow him through the Atlantic nightly: "It was something extravagantly abnormal. The distorted ball of the moon, the eerie half-light, the monstrous cloud shapes, the fog below and around us, the misty indefiniteness of space, the changeless drone, drone of the engines."

PRINCESS LOWENSTEIN-WERTHEIM

Princess Lowenstein-Wertheim was sixty. She was determined not only to be the first woman across the Atlantic, but to do it the hard way, from east to west, against westerly winds.

On August 31st, 1927, she and two experienced British airmen, Minchin and Hamilton, took off from the Salisbury Plain in England and set a course for Montreal. Halfway across their lights were spotted in the night sky by an oil tanker and—like many of the early flights—they were never seen again.

On the morning of April 13th they ran into Newfoundland fog banks and lost track of where they were. Worried about fuel, they suddenly saw a light. Thinking it was a ship, they circled and identified it as a lighthouse on a snow covered island. Kohl tried a hazardous landing and the undercarriage collapsed, but everybody survived.

The place was Greenly Island, north of Newfoundland, 1,000 miles from New York. But this was the first successful east-west crossing against the prevailing winds—it took 36$\frac{1}{2}$ hours.

CHARLES LINDBERGH

"My first indication of land was a fleet of fishing boats. I circled once and saw a man's face. I circled again and closing the throttle as the plane passed within a few feet of the boat, I shouted: 'Which way is Ireland?'" He was flying the purpose built "Spirit of St. Louis" non-stop across the Atlantic from New York to Paris and he was the first to do it alone.

Lindbergh took no chances. He waited for the perfect weather forecast and a full moon; he had a good aircraft and his instruments were far better than those of earlier pilots. But he had no radio and no navigator—he preferred the extra weight in fuel.

Like many of the early pilots the mystery of the Atlantic sky had a profound effect on Lindbergh. "Numerous shorelines

FIRST IRISHMAN TO FLY THE ATLANTIC

There were no German Pilots ever lost over the Atlantic. It was the English speaking nations who brushed aside bad weather forecasts, ignored pleas of "Don't go", revved up the tiny engines of frail aircraft, smiled, waved, took-off—and vanished.

The first Irishman to cross the ocean, James Fitzmaurice, went with two Germans, Baron von Hünefeld and Captain Hermann Kohl. They set off from Dublin on the 12th April 1928 intending to fly to New York. The pilots took three-hour stints.

appeared with trees perfectly outlined against the horizon. In fact, the mirages were so natural that had I not been in mid-Atlantic and known that no land existed along my route, I would have taken them to be actual islands."

The Spirit of St. Louis landed in Paris on the 21st May 1927 and Lindbergh, a quiet unassuming man, became a hero. He got 3$\frac{1}{2}$ million letters, several thousand offers of marriage, 5,000 poems, 1,400 gift parcels and three invitations to go to the moon in a rocket.

"I saw the green hills of Ireland and I knew that I had hit Europe on the nose. Ireland is one of the four corners of the world."

Above Left: Alcock and Brown and spectators in St. John's, Newfoundland, 1919.
Above Right: Col. Lindburgh and his wife Ann Morrow Lindbergh

The Hindenburg — moments after catching fire, May 6th, 1937

Short S.30 Cabot, under command of Kelly Rodgers, being refuelled in mid-air over Foynes by Handley Page HP.54 Harrow G-AFRL

THE NORTH ATLANTIC HAS SOME OF THE WORST AND MOST UNPREDICTABLE WEATHER IN THE WORLD. THE BIGGEST PROBLEM FACING THE AIRLINES WHO WANTED TO FLY COMMERCIALLY OVER THE LUCRATIVE ROUTES BETWEEN THE UNITED STATES AND EUROPE WAS THE VEHICLE. HOW COULD ONE AIRCRAFT CARRY PASSENGERS, FREIGHT AND ENOUGH FUEL TO FLY OVER 2,000 MILES IN SUCH TERRIBLE CONDITIONS?

AIRSHIPS

It was generally agreed in 1924 that the aeroplane would never be a suitable vehicle for carrying passengers across the Atlantic and that airships would operate all the long distance routes of the future.

In the summer of 1936, Germany began the first commercially viable service across the Atlantic using airships. These lighter than air balloons filled with highly flammable hydrogen gas were the slow moving, luxury liners of the sky.

In October 1930, the British Airship, the R100, crashed into a hillside in France and burst into flames. Of 54 people on board there were only six survivors.

Then on the 6th May, 1937, the German airship the Hindenberg, caught fire while mooring at New Jersey. The airship was completely destroyed and thirty-six people died. The whole disaster was recorded in vivid detail by a Pathe news film cameraman and reporter. The newsreel was shown in cinemas around the world.

After the accident, the other German airship, the Graf Zeppelin, was immediately withdrawn from the service— though it had a spotless safety record. There were no more airships on the Atlantic.

AIRPLANES

With airships proving to be slow and dangerous, attention turned to airplanes. Land planes were inappropriate as they were heavy and required hard runways—and there were very few of them before World War II.

On the other hand, flying boats had many advantages. There were always landing places for even the heaviest flying boat and almost all the great cities of the world were near the sea or large waterways—few had suitable runways. Because flying boats were not restricted to short runways, they could be bigger and much more luxurious. Also in the flying boats favour was the belief of the public—somewhat naively—that flying boats were safer when flying over water.

However, there were some problems with flying boats—they needed large amounts of fuel just to get itself off the water yet, once airborne they needed only a relatively small amount to keep it at a cruising speed. How do you get the aircraft into the air without using too much fuel? There were three initial answers to this question:

1. CATAPULTS

The German airline Lufthansa decided to try a novel solution. They would simply fling a seaplane from the deck of a depot ship using a compressed air catapult.

The parent ships dragged a large canvas apron behind them. The seaplane landed on the water, taxied over the apron and was lifted on board; oil was poured onto the sea to calm it. When the seaplane was refueled, it was shot into the sky.

Though this was successfully tried in 1937, it could never be used for passenger traffic because of the high gravity forces.

2. THE MAYO COMPOSITE

Another way to get an aircraft into the air without using fuel is on the back of another aircraft "piggy-back" style.

On the 20th July, 1938, the Short-Mayo Composite (designed by Major R.M. Mayo of Imperial Airways) took off from Foynes. The mother aircraft "Maia", carried the smaller "Mercury" well out to sea before they separated. After separation the Mercury flew on to Montreal and the Maia returned to Foynes.

The Mercury set three records:

• The first commercial Atlantic airmail flight.

• The first east/west crossing from Foynes to Montreal.

• The fastest time for an east/west crossing of the Atlantic.

But this would have been a dangerous and alarming way to handle passengers, and, as with in-flight refuelling, only mail could be carried. In 1939 the British Air ministry rejected the project.

3. IN-FLIGHT REFUELING

If an aircraft takes off under its own power, it uses a lot of its fuel just to get airborne. So, if it can refuel after takeoff, it can fly much further.

The only way to refuel in the air, of course, is from a flying petrol tanker. And this is exactly what British Imperial Airways tried in 1939.

Two flying boats—Cabot and Caribou—made eight round trips from Foynes to Newfoundland. They were refueled in the air by a converted Harrow bomber, which took off from the grass runway at Rineanna—which is now Shannon Airport.

A cable from the tanker was shot to the flying boat using a rocket-propelled harpoon. This was attached to a hose that was then locked into the flying boat's fuel tank; the tanker flew over the flying boat and the fuel flowed by gravity.

In the end, in July 1936, Pan American Airways signed a contract with Boeing for the first practical transatlantic passenger aircraft—the B.314 flying boat.

Top: The Catapult system. Middle: Imperial Airways Short S.30 Caribou
Above: The Maia and the Mercury being coupled to create the Mayo Composite

Weather

Crossing the Atlantic was a great challenge

"The North Atlantic is technically the most difficult operation of any major aerial route", Juan Trippe, President of Pan Am Airways.

Today, modern jet aircraft can fly above the weather and—except for takeoff and landing—are mostly unaffected by bad weather conditions. But flying boats often had to fly through or around storm clouds.

From October to May snow blocked the flying boat base at Botwood in Newfoundland. This made it necessary to re-route many of the winter flights via Lisbon, the Azores or even further south, via West Africa and South America.

Ice which formed on the wings or engines of flying boats could be very dangerous; it often completely blocked the windscreen and affected the radio equipment. Rubber de-icing boots were later fitted to the wings and tails of flying boats. Meteorologists also helped to choose flight plans to avoid severe icing.

It might often rain for the whole trip across the North Atlantic. Navigation on flying boats was mostly by "shooting" the sun, moon and stars, using a sextant— the instrument used on old sailing ships. Measurements were taken through a hatch at the top of the flying boat. Navigators used smoke floats dropped into the sea, to measure the effects of cross winds.

Except for short distances, radio contact was all by Morse code. Long distance voice communication was not possible until nearly 1950.

Although it is difficult to fly in cloud, the ceiling was often so low over the Atlantic that to fly under it would have been a danger to shipping.

There is an almost constant westerly wind on the Atlantic. For an aircraft flying from Canada to Ireland, this can be helpful, but a flying boat from Foynes to Botwood could be reduced to half speed or less by the winds. This often forced flights to turn back.

There is often a thirty-foot swell in the Atlantic. This would soon break up any flying boat that landed in an emergency.

THE POINT OF NO RETURN

This was the point after which the flying boat would not have had enough fuel to turn back, and flying boats often had to return to Foynes.

On one occasion an aircraft returned to Foynes after flying for 12 hours. One of the passengers who had slept for the whole flight saw the BOAC traffic officer and said "Good heavens, there's a chap exactly like you who saw us off at Foynes."

Top: Sean McWilliams, Met Staff, with a Dobson Ozone Spectrophotometer, taken opposite the Airport Terminal Building.

THE FIRST
PROVING FLIGHTS

Proving flights, or survey flights, were initial flights designed to test the ability of aircraft and the viability of certain routes to ascertain the costs for running the route in a commercial capacity. Generally being the first flight on the route meant the flight was going to have a number of risks attached to it—testing the limited range of engines, navigating over open featureless expanses of water, unpredictable and often bad weather and finding routes of acceptable commercial length.

On the evening of Thursday 25th February 1937 Foynes saw its first Flying Boat when Imperial Airways "Cambria" touched down shortly after 5pm under the command of Captain Powell having left Southampton at 1.48pm that afternoon on an experimental flight.

The next stage of experimental flights was held up as Imperial Airways and Pan American could not agree on who should be first to cross the North Atlantic. So it was decided that the first experimental crossings would be flown simultaneously in July 1937.

The westbound trip left Foynes on the 5th July, operated by Imperial Airways, Short S-23C 'Caledonia' under Capt. A. S. Wilcockson. Éamon de Valera travelled to Foynes to see the flight off.

On the 5th July 1937 First Survey flight by Pan Am's Sikorsky 'Clipper III' under command of Captain Harold Gray and his crew of six; N.S. de Lima, William M. Masland, Walter Smith, H.J. Roberts, C.D. Wright and William Thaler, departed Botwood Newfoundland for Foynes.

After 12 hours and 31 minutes, they arrived in Foynes. They departed Botwood with 2,350 gallons of fuel on board and still had 900 gallons left on arrival at Foynes. They were welcomed by Éamon de Valera, President of the Executive Council, Sean Lemass, Minister for Industry and Commerce and Sean Leydon, Secretary at the Department of Industry and Commerce.

Lemass and Leydon had responsibility for all the ports in Ireland, of which Foynes was one of the most important and under the Civil Aviation Section, the Department also had responsibility for the flying boat base at Foynes. De Valera throughout his life showed a keen interest in aviation and in 1936, was taken on a flight by Colonel Charles Lindbergh from Baldonnell.

The Clipper III left Foynes the following day, Thursday July 8th at 9am for Southampton and was seen off by Colonel Charles Lindbergh, who had flown to Ireland on 7th July.

Both companies conducted many more survey flights during 1937 and 1938. The most unusual flight was the Mayo Composite operated by Imperial Airways. Imperial were having difficulties providing aircraft with enough fuel capacity to cross the Atlantic and asked their designer Major Mayo to come up with a solution.

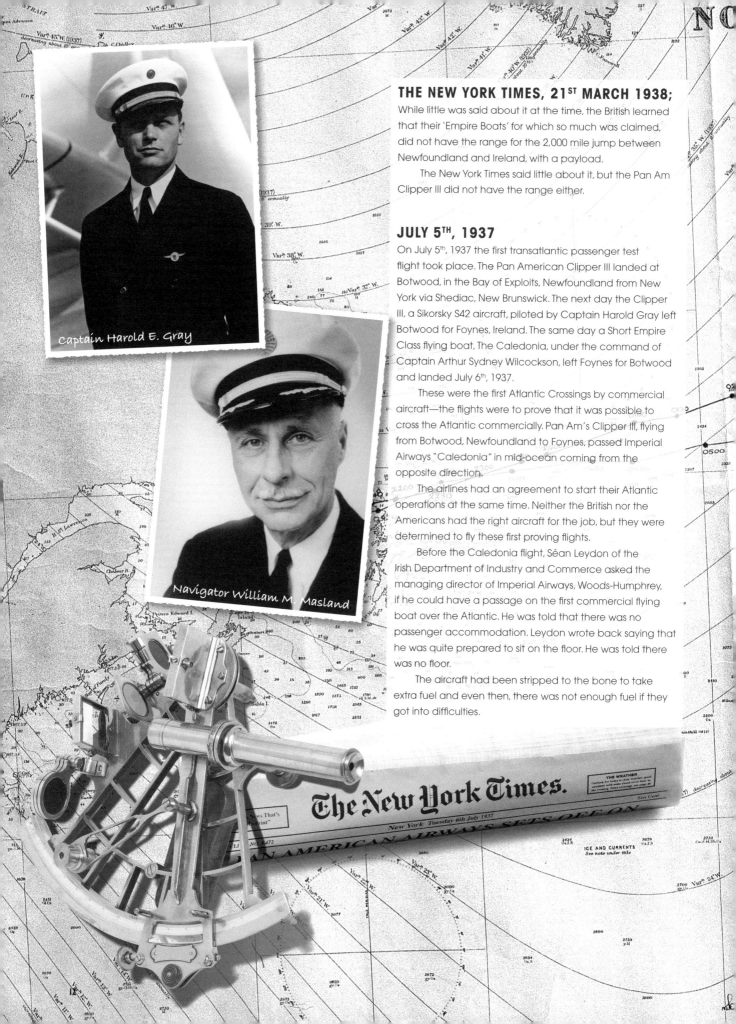

Captain Harold E. Gray

Navigator William M. Masland

THE NEW YORK TIMES, 21ST MARCH 1938;

While little was said about it at the time, the British learned that their 'Empire Boats' for which so much was claimed, did not have the range for the 2,000 mile jump between Newfoundland and Ireland, with a payload.

The New York Times said little about it, but the Pan Am Clipper III did not have the range either.

JULY 5TH, 1937

On July 5th, 1937 the first transatlantic passenger test flight took place. The Pan American Clipper III landed at Botwood, in the Bay of Exploits, Newfoundland from New York via Shediac, New Brunswick. The next day the Clipper III, a Sikorsky S42 aircraft, piloted by Captain Harold Gray left Botwood for Foynes, Ireland. The same day a Short Empire Class flying boat, The Caledonia, under the command of Captain Arthur Sydney Wilcockson, left Foynes for Botwood and landed July 6th, 1937.

These were the first Atlantic Crossings by commercial aircraft—the flights were to prove that it was possible to cross the Atlantic commercially. Pan Am's Clipper III, flying from Botwood, Newfoundland to Foynes, passed Imperial Airways "Caledonia" in mid-ocean coming from the opposite direction.

The airlines had an agreement to start their Atlantic operations at the same time. Neither the British nor the Americans had the right aircraft for the job, but they were determined to fly these first proving flights.

Before the Caledonia flight, Séan Leydon of the Irish Department of Industry and Commerce asked the managing director of Imperial Airways, Woods-Humphrey, if he could have a passage on the first commercial flying boat over the Atlantic. He was told that there was no passenger accommodation. Leydon wrote back saying that he was quite prepared to sit on the floor. He was told there was no floor.

The aircraft had been stripped to the bone to take extra fuel and even then, there was not enough fuel if they got into difficulties.

The New York Times.
New York Tuesday 6th July 1937
PAN AMERICAN AIRWAYS SETS OFF ON

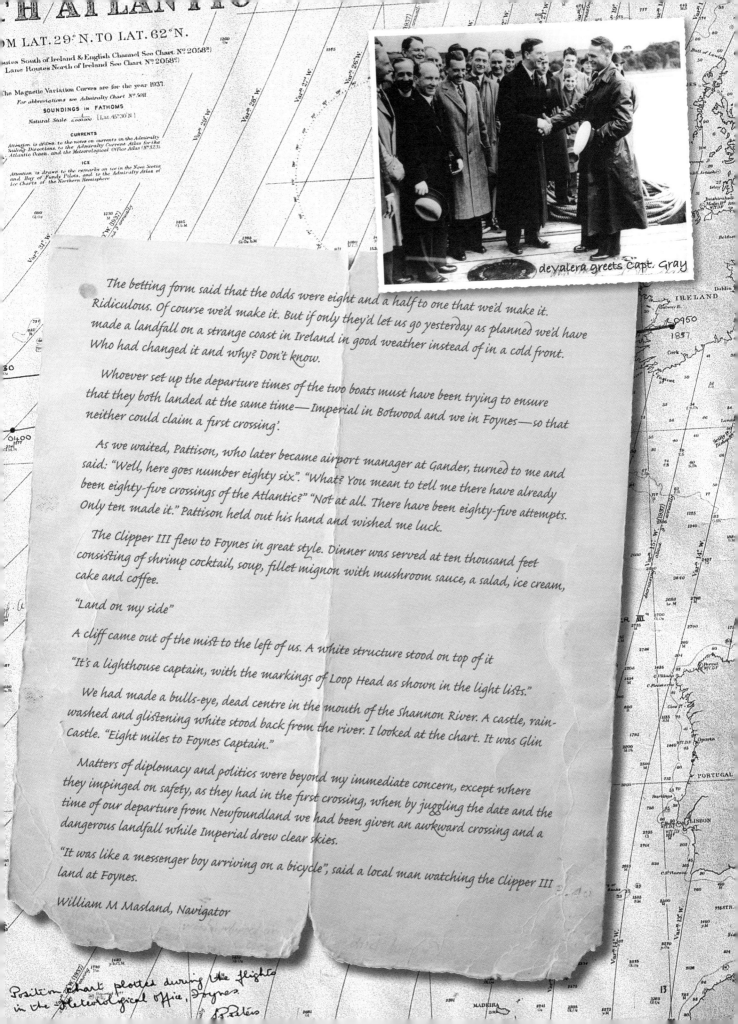

de valera greets Capt. Gray

The betting form said that the odds were eight and a half to one that we'd make it. Ridiculous. Of course we'd make it. But if only they'd let us go yesterday as planned we'd have made a landfall on a strange coast in Ireland in good weather instead of in a cold front. Who had changed it and why? Don't know.

Whoever set up the departure times of the two boats must have been trying to ensure that they both landed at the same time—Imperial in Botwood and we in Foynes—so that neither could claim a first crossing.

As we waited, Pattison, who later became airport manager at Gander, turned to me and said: "Well, here goes number eighty six". "What? You mean to tell me there have already been eighty-five crossings of the Atlantic?" "Not at all. There have been eighty-five attempts. Only ten made it." Pattison held out his hand and wished me luck.

The Clipper III flew to Foynes in great style. Dinner was served at ten thousand feet consisting of shrimp cocktail, soup, fillet mignon with mushroom sauce, a salad, ice cream, cake and coffee.

"Land on my side"

A cliff came out of the mist to the left of us. A white structure stood on top of it

"It's a lighthouse captain, with the markings of Loop Head as shown in the light lists."

We had made a bulls-eye, dead centre in the mouth of the Shannon River. A castle, rain-washed and glistening white stood back from the river. I looked at the chart. It was Glin Castle. "Eight miles to Foynes Captain."

Matters of diplomacy and politics were beyond my immediate concern, except where they impinged on safety, as they had in the first crossing, when by juggling the date and the time of our departure from Newfoundland we had been given an awkward crossing and a dangerous landfall while Imperial drew clear skies.

"It was like a messenger boy arriving on a bicycle", said a local man watching the Clipper III land at Foynes.

William M Masland, Navigator

Position chart plotted during the flights
in the Meteorological office, Foynes
B. Peters

Imperial Airways Short S.23 'Caledonia', being serviced by Irish Shell. First man standing on left with hands on hips is Paddy Walsh, next man standing with hands on hips also, is Mick Walsh. Man on extreme right standing in Boat is Michael Hanley.

THE IRISH TIMES, 6TH JULY, 1937:
Caledonia heads for Canada

"The engines roared into life and Caledonia moved slowly down the Channel between the mainland and Foynes Island. As it passed the quayside, a cheer broke from the great crowd. Suddenly, the noise of the engines changed into a terrific roar as the full force of their 3,600 horsepower came into action. Spray dashed over the great 114 foot span of its wings as the flying boat ploughed forward. Just 40 seconds after the throttle opened, Caledonia left the water and disappeared towards Kerry Head and the Ocean. Its transatlantic flight had begun.

Wilcockson was the Captain of the Imperial Airway's Caledonia. "I slipped moorings at 18:42GMT. It was raining, with low cloud and a 30mph wind. Not all the sort of night for a jaunt of this description. I taxied round the western end of Foynes Island and took off diagonally across the river. The takeoff was good and I put the aircraft direct on course for Loop Head and Botwood."

Half way across, Caledonia saw the ship SS Empress of Britain. A star sight of Jupiter and Arcturus shortly afterwards put the flying boat 22 miles south of course, before continuous rain enveloped them.

At 00:45 we came out of the fog at 2,500 feet and saw the sun rise over the cloud layers. Caledonia landed at 10:15, 15 hours and 25 minutes after leaving Foynes.

'Caledonia' crew being greeted at Foynes by Eamon deValera with (L-R) Thomas Adams Valette, Capt. Arthur Sidney Wilcockson, Charles Henry Bowes and Thomas Eric Hobbs

INAUGURAL AIR MAIL

On June 28th, 1939, Pan Am's Yankee Clipper landed at Foynes. It was the first scheduled airmail flight on the "Great Circle" route across the North Atlantic. The Great Circle route is the direct route from Newfoundland to Ireland. It is the fastest and most important flight path from the American continent to Europe.

On Wednesday 28th June, 1939 the "Yankee Clipper" under the command of Capt. Harold Gray, arrived in Foynes with 18 invited guests and 11 crew on board including Juan Trippe, Pan Am's famous President. 14 bags of mail were also on board, the first transatlantic airmail to arrive in Foynes from the United States.

The first fare paying passengers across the direct route landed at Foynes on July 9th, 1939. The flying boat was again the Yankee Clipper. There were 19 passengers and a crew of 12 led by Captain Arthur E. La Porte.

The Clipper left Botwood at 11.30pm on Saturday night 8th July 1939 and appeared over Foynes at 12.50pm on Sunday 9th July. There was a rousing cheer for the 19 passengers from the crowd on the quayside. Even though these passenger services were now available to all comers, they were not cheap—$375 single and $675 return.

Imperial Airways were still trying to find a solution to their problem of not having aircraft capable of carrying enough fuel to make the Atlantic Crossing and to compete with Pan Am's Boeing 314s.

A new system of refueling aircraft in mid air was to be tried. Sir Alan Cobham began experiments on refueling aircraft in mid air.

On Saturday 5th August 1939 Imperial Airways "Caribou" under the command of Captain J.C. Kelly Rogers arrived in Foynes on route to New York carrying 1,000 lbs of mail to inaugurate their North Atlantic service.

The Caribou was refueled in mid-air over Foynes and then flew on to Botwood where it was again refueled in mid-air before continuing it's flight to New York via Montreal. No passengers were allowed on this flight only mail. The system was used eight times through Foynes but was then abandoned.

1939 had been a hectic year at Foynes but with the outbreak of World War 2 on September 3rd 1939 Pan Am announced that all future services to Southampton were cancelled and that the Neutral port of Foynes would be the new terminal where the flights would turn around.

Throughout the War Years scheduled services continued across the Atlantic using Foynes as their eastern terminal on the northern route. Although these services were flown by civilian airlines in reality they supported the war effort. Pan Ams last flight departed Foynes in October 1939 and it was May 1942 before Pan Am re-appeared in Foynes.

The first mails to arrive in Foynes. Locals included in the photo are Eddie McCarthy (in white overalls) and Alfie Litle. Between 1939 and 1943, 150,876lbs of mail were loaded onto and 197,318lbs off-loaded from flying boats at Foynes.

In July 1940 American Export airlines received their licence to operate on the Atlantic. Charles F. Blair was appointed Chief Pilot and on the 28th May 1942 their first flight arrived in Foynes from New York under Captain Blair, thus beginning a long association with Foynes and later Shannon for Captain Blair.

In June 1942 the Sikorsky S-44 "Excalibur" captained by Charles Blair made the first non-stop flight of the Atlantic with passengers and mail. Departing Foynes 22nd June and arriving 25 hours and 40 minutes later on Flushing Bay, New York. In October 1944 Captain Blair completed the fastest flying boat crossing of the Atlantic in 14 hrs. and 17min. for the 3,100 mile flight from New York to Foynes.

WESTERN UNION

1201

Class of Service

This is a full-rate Telegram or Cablegram unless its deferred character is indicated by a suitable symbol above or preceding the address.

R. B. WHITE PRESIDENT

NEWCOMB CARLTON CHAIRMAN OF THE BOARD

J. C. WILLEVER FIRST VICE-PRESIDENT

SYMBOLS

DL = Day Letter
NL = Night Letter
LC = Deferred Cable
NLT = Cable Night Letter
Ship Radiogram

The filing time shown in the data line on telegrams and day letters is STANDARD TIME at point of origin. Time of receipt is STANDARD TIME at point of destination

Release to book a

Tws paid

Portwashington June 27 -- the Pan American Airways flying boat Yankee Clipper, enroute to Europe with inaugural airmail over the "northern" route via Canada, Newfoundland, and Ireland to England, took off from Shediac, New Brunswick, at 13.49 PM edst today for Botwood, Newfoundland, last stop before the 1,995 mile ocean crossing to Ireland. The clipper has been delayed at Shediac since Saturday, due to unusually severe fog conditions over Newfoundland.

Northeast winds blowing off the Greenland ice cap produced fog at Botwood intermittantly for three days, and prudency dictated the delay of the schedule at Shediac until this condition cleared. The clipper is carrying, in addition to a record mail load of 2,532 pounds, 20 official government and Pan American Airways observers.

··· APPRECIATE SUGGESTIONS FROM ITS PATRONS CONCERNING ITS SERVICE

WESTERN UNION

1312

Class of Service

This is a full-rate Telegram or Cablegram unless its deferred character is indicated by a suitable symbol above or preceding the address.

R. B. WHITE PRESIDENT

NEWCOMB CARLTON CHAIRMAN OF THE BOARD

J. C. WILLEVER FIRST VICE-PRESIDENT

SYMBOLS

DL = Day Letter
NL = Night Letter
LC = Deferred Cable
NLT = Cable Night Letter
Ship Radiogram

The filing time shown in the data line on telegrams and day letters is STANDARD TIME at point of origin. Time of receipt is STANDARD TIME at point of destination

Release to book a.

Tws paid

Portwashington June 27 -- a radiogram from Yankee Clipper at 2:10 this morning told of a gay birthday party high above the clouds in mid-Atlantic as the great 41-ton Pan American Airways flying boat sped eastward to Europe on the inaugural airmail flight to England via Canada, Newfoundland and Ireland. The group of government observers aboard the clipper, headed by under secretary of state R. Walton Moore and Clinton Hester, administrator of the civil aeronautics authority, discovered that today June 27 was the birthday of Juan T. Trippe, president of Pan American Airways, who is host to the group on their european flight. So immediately after midnight the group staged a mid-Atlantic birthday party, everyone managing to find some sort of present for the airline head. Everyone expressed admiration for Mr. Trippe's leadership in establishing the first transatlantic air service to Europe.

THE COMPANY WILL APPRECIATE SUGGESTIONS FROM ITS PATRONS CONCERNING ITS SERVICE

WESTERN UNION

1221

R. B. WHITE
PRESIDENT

NEWCOMB CARLTON
CHAIRMAN OF THE BOARD

J. C. WILLEVER
FIRST VICE-PRESIDENT

The filing time shown in the data line on telegrams and day letters is STANDARD TIME at point of origin. Time of receipt is STANDARD TIME at point of destination

Release to book a.

Tws paid

Portwashington June 28-- at 12:30 am edst today, capt. Harold E. Gray aboard the Pan American Airways flying boat Yankee Clipper reported his position as 583 miles northeast of Botwood, Newfoundland, bound for Foynes, Ireland. Meanwhile the birthday party for Mr. Trippe was in full swing as the clipper began to climb to higher altitude for more favourable winds aloft.

Pan American Airways...100a

THE COMPANY WILL APPRECIAT

WESTERN UNION

1602

R. B. WHITE
PRESIDENT

NEWCOMB CARLTON
CHAIRMAN OF THE BOARD

J. C. WILLEVER
FIRST VICE-PRESIDENT

The filing time shown in the data line on telegrams and day letters is STANDARD TIME at point of origin. Time of receipt is STANDARD TIME at point of destination

Release to book a.

Tws paid

Portwashington June 28-- at 5:30 am edst this morning Yankie Clipper, enroute to Europe, was 1,320 miles east of Botwood, with only 675 miles yet to go to Foynes, Ireland. The clipper was flying at 8,000 feet.

Pan American Airways....607a

WESTERN UNION

1554

R. B. WHITE
PRESIDENT

NEWCOMB CARLTON
CHAIRMAN OF THE BOARD

J. C. WILLEVER
FIRST VICE-PRESIDENT

PATRONS CONCERNING ITS SERVICE

The filing time shown in the data line on telegrams and day letters is STANDARD TIME at point of origin. Time of receipt is STANDARD TIME at point of destination

Release to book a.

Tws paid

Portwashington June 28-- Yankee Clipper, bound for Europe over the "northern" route to England via Canada, Newfoundland and Ireland, was 1,058 miles east of Botwood, Newfoundland, at 3:30 am edst this morning. She was flying at 7,800 feet over a solid layer of cloud, with a moderate wind from due north on her port beam.

Pan American Airways....410 A

The Radio Room in the Foynes Airport Terminal Building

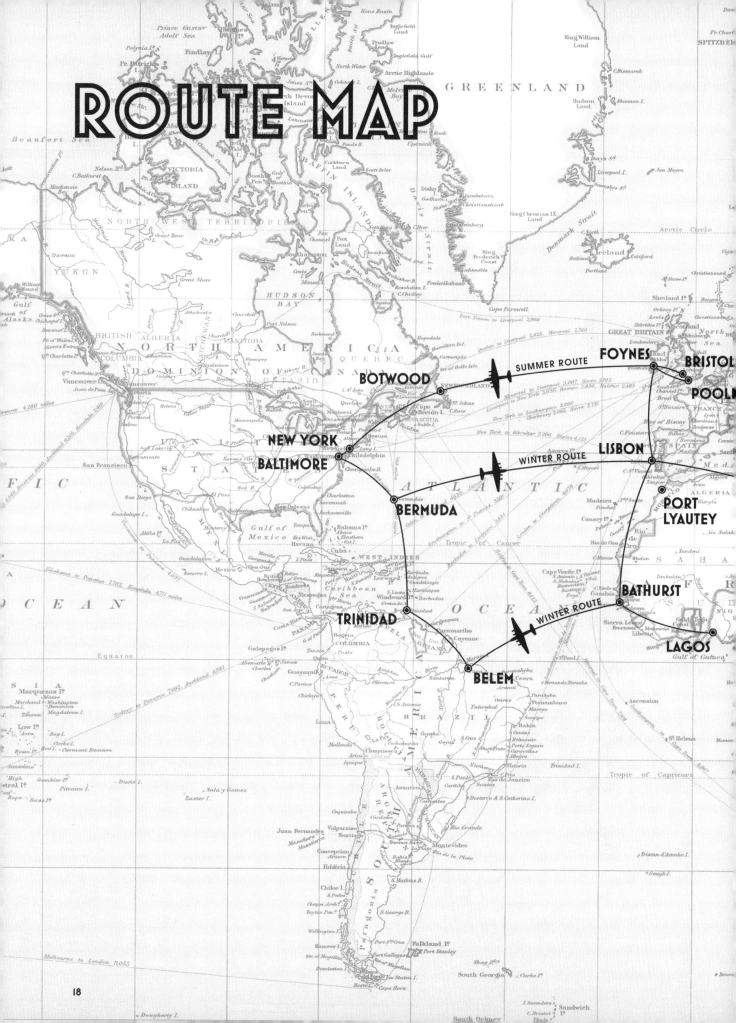

ROUTE MAP

BOTWOOD

SUMMER ROUTE

FOYNES

BRISTOL

POOLE

NEW YORK

BALTIMORE

WINTER ROUTE

LISBON

PORT LYAUTEY

BERMUDA

BATHURST

TRINIDAD

WINTER ROUTE

LAGOS

BELEM

CAIRO

19

FOYNES TO NEW YORK NONSTOP

FIRST TIME WITH PASSENGERS

Captain Charles Blair, an extract from his book, *Red Ball in the Sky*, © 1952

'WE SET OUT FROM FOYNES ON THIS LONGEST OF THE SUMMER DAYS, WITHOUT ANY SPECIAL AMBITION. THE BIG SIKORSKY'S FUEL TANKS WERE A FEW HUNDRED GALLONS SHORT OF THEIR 3,820 GALLON CAPACITY WHEN THE SEAPLANE SLIPPED HER MOORING TO EASE INTO THE RIPTIDE THAT RACED THROUGH THE NARROW WEST CHANNEL BETWEEN FOYNES ISLAND AND THE SOUTH BANK OF THE SHANNON. THE FLIGHT PLAN CALLED FOR A FUEL STOP AT BOTWOOD IN NEWFOUNDLAND ON THE BAY OF EXPLOITS—SOME FOURTEEN HOURS AWAY.

An onlooker on the shore might have thought this heavily leaden flying boat was more likely to go to the bottom of the broad river rather than fly safely across the ocean. The hull was so deeply submerged by the full load that the passenger windows were only inches above water level.

At the beginning of takeoff a huge wave flared out from the bow to enshroud the ship so heavily with spray that only the wing tips and top of the tail were visible. Finally, seeking release from its briny surroundings, the hull lumbered heavily onto the step at a mile a minute clip and began to skim across the water toward its hundred mile an hour takeoff speed.

On this cool June evening a brisk west wind streaked the waters of Ireland's fabled River Shannon. I pulled back strenuously on the controls as Excalibur climbed quickly into hydroplaning position, then swept majestically down river toward Loop Head and the North Atlantic.

On this voyage my crew was unusually heavy with airline wisdom. Along for some practical training were four senior airline captains whose total flying experience probably exceeded any like grouping ever before assembled on a flight deck. In the co-pilot's seat was Captain Bob Hixson, one of the best aviators I know and a veteran of United's transcontinental. Hixson had a head start over the others. He had been flying with me during the S-44 tests at Jacksonville and had already been fully purged of any inclination toward land planes.

Sixteen passengers occupied the Sikorsky's spacious passenger cabin— two to each stateroom. They included Britain's famed combat admiral and commander of the Mediterranean Fleet, Sir Andrew Cunningham. The admiral was on his way to Washington to help arrange the invasion of North Africa. Along, too, were a couple of ambassadors and some other top brass. The host in the passenger cabin was purser Bill Scouler, a miniature Scot who was assisted by stewardess Doroty Bohanna, R.N.—the first stewardess to fly any ocean.

This first scheduled westbound flight of American Export Airlines promised to be a long voyage, but the passenger accommodations were much more plush than those of the latter-day land planes. Nor did the crew members suffer. We could take turns easing the fatigue problem in the berths up forward, below the flight deck.

Although there was a war going on, most of our ocean-flying hazards stemmed from the winds and weather. However, later in the war, when flying closer to Europe across the Bay of Biscay to and from Portugal and North Africa, there would be occasional fireworks from a German submarine.

But I was shot at only once during three years of wartime flying. This was to the west of Lisbon, in the early dawn and the submariners may have been as surprised as we were. But they had the ammunition, and we had none.

The enemy fighter-interceptors never bothered any of the flying boats, although some British land plane airliners were less lucky. Our ocean-hugging flying boats always managed to hide from hostile radar eyes scanning the Bay of Biscay from the coastline of France and Spain.

There was little man-made trouble in the air over the North Atlantic, but we sometimes encountered victims of well-aimed torpedoes burning fiercely on the surface of the windblown ocean, lighting up the night for miles around.

On this particular June night the war seemed to be elsewhere. Excalibur rumbled peacefully through the darkness a thousand feet above the sea. The only evidence of the ocean's presence was the faint luminescence of wind-tossed whitecaps which appeared vaguely as tumbling crescents unfolding toward the westerlies that created them.

"A SKY-FULL OF STARS TOLD US EXACTLY WHERE WE WERE"

The big hull, suspended from a wide span of wing, occasionally trembled slightly in the ripple of wind and cloud, but at a hundred and thirty knots on the airspeed indicator there was no discomfort in this gentle motion. On the flight deck Harry Lamont was in charge of navigation, and his first concern was to guarantee accurate course. Now and then he made his way aft toward the stern where he would toss out a smoke bomb that would burn on the surface of the sea to allow the measurement of drift.

We dead reckoned below the clouds until past mid-ocean, using only the airspeed, compass and drift flares for guidance. But dead reckoning wasn't enough. More exact information was needed, which called for a glimpse of the heavens. So, though it cost some fuel, we struggled up to eight thousand feet, where a sky-full of stars told us exactly where we were.

Mike Doyle, the chief flight engineer, kept himself awake matching his fuel records against the navigational score. An effervescent Irishman with a twinkle in the eye and a gray fringe around his bald head, Mike exuded great physical power. He was short and stocky, and sturdy as a fire hydrant.

This seagoing craftsman and retired chief aviation machinist mate had learned his trade during a twenty-three-year hitch in the Navy. Along with his airborne duties, he was capable of fixing anything that needed to be fixed on a flying boat—from splicing a line or mending a hole in the bottom to changing an engine at a windblown, wave-tossed mooring.

There was little to disturb the stillness of the night watch except the chatter of the radio operator's transmitting bug which sputtered Morse Code into the four corners of the ocean. While on duty all radio operators seem like men from another planet, withdrawn into a world of their own which speaks a twittering language of dashes and dots.

On this trip Mike McFarlen was chief radio operator. A slim and dour Texan, Mike's usually solemn face could flash an engaging smile when things were going right. But his face

The radio operator was merely saying out loud what I had been thinking during the past few hours. Where could we take on some gasoline?

Beyond Newfoundland the next seaplane base that boasted a fueling barge was at Shediac in the Canadian Maritimes. Shediac, near Moncton in New Brunswick was a first-class haven for flying boats. But our weather messages indicated this harbour, too, would be heavily fogged-in during the hours we could use it.

American Export VS44-A 'Excalibur' NC 41880 in flight over Foynes. In 1942, the 'Excalibur' under the command of Capt. Charles Blair did the first transatlantic non-stop flight with passengers and mail. The flight from Foynes to New York took 25 hours and 40 minutes

was more solemn than usual. His deep pile of radio messages describing the threatening weather in Newfoundland gave him nothing to smile about. I noticed his long, thin face become more melancholy.

"Skipper, its going to be socked in", McFarlen finally announced in a mournful twang.

The surface wind at Botwood, where we were scheduled to land for fuel, had veered to the northeast, blowing in a blanket of drizzle and fog from the ocean, covering Botwood's Bay of Exploits and the alternate landing area at Gander Lake.

Halifax, therefore, was the final resort, although there was nothing certain about this harbour on Nova Scotia's east coast. Yet the fog there would surely be thinned into less troublesome smog by the steepening rays of the summer sun. There should be enough visibility for a safe landing.

Because Newfoundland was clearly a lost cause, we altered course a few degrees left to pass seaward of Cape Race as its southeastern tip. For several hours we had been soaring smoothly above softly luminous clouds under a canopy of stars, lapping up the luxury of precise celestial navigation.

But this easygoing flying above the clouds was courting trouble. A reddish pinpoint of light in the western sky was gradually telling us we were encountering some forceful resistance. Aldebaran, the red star hanging directly over Excalibur's nose between a dimly lit Pleiades and the gaudy spread of Orion, was sensing an intolerable headwind that would bite deeply into our fuel reserves.

"These speed lines show we've made thirty miles in the last thirty minutes," Harry Lamont declared glumly. 'That means we've got 80 knots on the nose. Our groundspeed is less than half our airspeed."

Mike Doyle pushed his pencil a few moments. "That's four-tenths of a mile per gallon, and we've got eleven hundred gallons."

"At that rate", I reckoned, "we'll have dry tanks a hundred miles short of Halifax."

"Glad this is a boat", said Hixson.

The only place to improve matters would be down near the surface of the sea. If the ground wind at Botwood was northeasterly, it shouldn't be too much different in the vicinity of Cape Race—which would give us a welcome tailwind.

Because our airplane undoubtedly owned a monopoly of this part of the ocean, McFarlen merely rattled off our intentions in a clatter of dashes and dots. Airway traffic control on the oceans hardly existed in those days.

With our new plan declared, we took leave of the hostile upper air, and quickly plunged into an envelopment of amorphous mist, which was soon harshened by the rising sun behind. As we felt our way down through the lowest layer of cloud, the blinding white mists turned into gray, and suddenly we were totally released from the sun-drenched glare to find ourselves beneath the clouds' lowest tendril only a few hundred feet above the blue-black ocean.

It was lucky we hadn't postponed this cloud penetration much longer because the leaden overcast soon sank almost to the tops of the long Atlantic swells. But even though the cloud ceiling was close to the surface of the ocean, we still had to fly high enough to elude the masts of small shipping that might suddenly appear in front of us.

It turned out there was none of the hoped-for northeasterly tailwind near the surface, but at least we were free of the ill-mannered headwinds that cost so much fuel. The Sikorsky rode smoothly along on a windless cushion of ocean air, and at this low altitude it was a bonanza worth a few drums of gasoline. The cushion of air between the flying boat's big wings and the surface of the sea allowed such a substantial reduction of fuel flow to our thirsty engines that the fuel records would surely agitate the slide rules of our engineering friends back home. We reduced the rpm's as low as we could and still stay efficiently airborne. The noise of propellers and engine became a whisper.

Excalibur skimmed over the swells, clocking one hundred and ten knots. The visibility ahead was scant, but it was enough. We felt secure in our knowledge that the big icebergs were astern, and that the tall cliffs of Cape Race would pass a comfortable distance to starboard. Nor was there much to worry about from big shipping. The big ocean vessels seldom cruised in this domain of the bluenose fisherman.

"THE ONLY PLACE TO IMPROVE MATTERS WOULD BE DOWN NEAR THE SURFACE OF THE SEA"

Flying close to the rolling swells demanded alert attention, and kept everyone on the flight deck wide-awake. The hours ground away in to monotonous infinity until we became hardly conscious of the sound of the engines. Finally, the windless sea was broken by a patch of rock-studded whitecaps.

"Land ho!" Hixon announced, much as Columbus must have said it on the poop deck of the Santa Maria.

For the huge continent of North America, it was certainly a niggardly landfall, but for us it was land. The northeastern cape of fog-smitten Nova Scotia was less than a mile away, yet it was totally invisible.

Although sandwiched tightly between cloud and ocean, we had enough visibility to dodge any obstruction that might loom ahead. Nor did the mists of the morning dampen a new prospect. At our first landfall we had as many gallons of fuel remaining as there were miles to go to New York. I was beginning to toy with the idea of flying non-stop.

The Pratt and Whitney engines churned smoothly at thirteen hundred revolutions per minute, burning a gallon of fuel for each nautical mile that slipped under the keel, and I knew that this fuel versus mileage factor would improve slightly as the airplane further unburdened its fuel tonnage.

We held course close to shore, but the only visible evidence of the low-lying coastline was an occasional sea-swept rock that jutted from the coastal shallows.

From Nova Scotia's northeastern promontory, it would be an hour and a half to Halifax, the last place before New York where we could get fuel out of a hose. The cloud ceiling at

Halifax was reported to be close to the surface of the sea, but this posed no difficult problem. We were already under the overcast. All we needed was a radio bearing when offshore the entrance to the harbor. Then we could turn and fly along it among the shipping to the landing area.

But there was a problem about Halifax that land plane pilots would scarcely appreciate. The bottom of the flying boat, being of thin metal, was vulnerable to floating debris. Three days ago, while eastbound, we paused at Halifax for extra fuel before undertaking the long flight to Ireland. The harbor was infested with a scattering of small pieces of lumber, which were barely visible above the greasy, glassy surface. During the landing and takeoff among a clutter of shipping it was necessary to swerve the big seaplane to right and left to escape the menacing debris.

This was a repelling consideration, and it conspired with our newly discovered fuel thrift. I was slowly abandoning the idea of landing anywhere short of New York.

We had been aloft twenty hours since the last glimpse of land at Loop Head near the mouth of the Shannon. Twenty hours of fuel records had to be thoroughly double checked before I could commit the Sikorsky to the five hour extension to New York.

"Mike," I said, 'let's recheck all those flow meter records since Foynes—double check 'em. Maybe we'll go all the way."

The engineer gave a questioning look, and then his eyes lit up, "Yes sir! I'll have it in a couple of minutes."

Hixon added his approval. 'Now you're talking, Charlie."

"Mac, get a reading on the Boston and New York Weather."

McFarlen flashed a smile for the first time in twenty hours. The flight deck came alive.

It turned out that the fuel records agreed with the less dependable fuel gauges, and we were clearly gaining a little on the fuel-versus-mile score. We now possessed a few more gallons of fuel than there were miles to go.

Our ace in the hole was a sight gauge full of gasoline. It was a vertical glass tube fastened to a hundred-gallon reserve tank above the aft end of the fight deck. This was the last tank we would be using, and it was reassuring to actually see the gasoline. When the fuel started descending in that glass tube we would fly one hundred miles more and that would be all.

I let Halifax slip invisibly by as if it wasn't there, but this didn't mean I was going for broke on this last lap to New York. There were various small harbors and a couple of big ones up ahead that could offer safe anchorage. I could even land safely in the open ocean without suffering any damage except to ego.

The idea of terminating the voyage anywhere between Halifax and New York was painful to contemplate. Our competitors would be greatly amused to see us put on an amateur performance. Even worse, although the high brass in the passenger cabin had been admirably cheerful thus far, the mood would certainly chill if we dropped down in some remote cove.

But if the westerly surface wind didn't freshen too much, the big S-44 would be setting a new transatlantic standard before she was fastened to her mooring at New York's marine terminal at La Guardia Airport.

New York's Whitestone Bridge was silhouetted beneath the afternoon sun when we switched to the tank that showed the final 100 gallons of fuel. Our press agents had been boasting for years about flying nonstop across the Atlantic. Now this was about to happen—the first time for an airliner with passengers and mail.

We climbed above the big span just to make sure everyone was aware this was an airplane, not a surface vessel—if anyone was beginning to wonder.

The fuel tank showed ninety-five gallons when Mike Doyle looped the mooring hawser around the bow post. This was enough, though it was only a tiny fraction of the gasoline we lifted off the River Shannon twenty-five hours and forty minutes before landing on Flushing Bay.

"Remarkable voyage", was the British Navy's crisp analysis when Admiral Cunningham disembarked, and the glint in his eye suggested he wasn't being loose with his praise.

But it would have been just another ocean flight with a fuel stop if that red star in the sky—Aldebaran—hadn't flagged us down out of the headwinds."

The New York City skyline in the 1930s

FOYNES AIRPORT

THE DAY TO DAY OPERATIONS OF FOYNES AIRPORT, OR SHANNON AIRPORT AS IT WAS THEN KNOW, DURING THE FLYING BOAT ERA OF 1939 TO 1945.

A Boeing 314 is due to arrive at Foynes 0700H on Wednesday from the United States. The aircraft is to leave again at around 1800H for Lisbon.

The arrival time of the 314 is uncertain because, until the actual day of departure, no one knows whether conditions will permit the flight via Botwood in Newfoundland or whether the longer routeing via Bermuda and the Azores will have to be chosen. And no one knows how long the flight will be likely to take until the wind forecasts are known. This arrival time is key to the whole operation. The crew that bring the aircraft in have to take it out in the evening as there is no slip crew.

At that time, British aircrew utilisation was more important than aircraft utilisation as all available crew were required for military service. Thus the evening departure of the 314 could only take place after the crew had sufficient rest. And there was no point in operating the shuttles until one knew a little more certainly that the 314 would, in fact, arrive and depart.

By about midday on Tuesday, forecasts for the Atlantic ocean area East of 30° West longitude, and landing forecasts for Foynes, Stranraer in Scotland and Poole in England are on the way by radio to Baltimore. Shortly after, a flight plan signal is received giving: routeing, times expected at key points along the route, an estimated time of arrival at Foynes at 0700H, and details of the expected load aboard.

Arrangements are made for traffic staff to be on duty at 0600H; for breakfasts to be available from 0800H for passengers and crew; for transport to take the 314 Captain to the Dunraven Arms at Adare and the rest of the crew to the Royal George in Limerick. The shuttles are confirmed to leave England at 0800H and to leave from Foynes and Rineanna respectively at 1200H and 1330H—and the operations staff settle down to monitor the process of the flight during the night.

By midnight it becomes obvious that the eastbound 314 is making better progress than had been expected, and it is likely to arrive at least an hour ahead of schedule, if not more. This could be a problem. If it is likely to be very much earlier and before daybreak there may be a need for a flarepath. If it is only an hour or so early this won't be necessary, but in any case it may be necessary to call in the traffic staff, together with Customs, Immigration and Police and the resident British and American security-cum-consular officials—both of whom lived as BOAC guests at Boland's Meadow. The majority of the others, however, live in a variety of dwellings scattered across the area and out of telephone contact.

As a precautionary measure the night duty launch crew is instructed to get the flarepath components ready.

By 0330H it becomes obvious that the aircraft will arrive at around 0600H which is after dawn has broken, so the flarepath components are returned to store. "Milo" the messenger is called and is sent out to alert staff to be on duty at 0500H.

Thirty minutes before the confirmed expected arrival time the control launches go out to check that the selected alighting area is free from other craft and drifting debris, while the BOAC launch goes out to make up the mooring.

By this time all staff are on duty, the buildings are open and lit, and preparations are under way for coffee, tea and biscuits to be available for the incoming crew and passengers as soon as they get ashore.

In the meantime operations staff have confirmed with BOAC Headquarters in England that the operation is proceeding normally and the shuttle operations are firmed up.

Foynes Island

As the passengers and their baggage are disembarked, the ground engineer gets a briefing on the aircraft from the flight engineer and takes over the Technical Log which contains instrument recordings made during the flight and a list of defects that may have occurred during it. During the day the ground engineers will rectify all the faults that may affect the safety of operations and as many of the others as they can. Some unimportant defects which do not affect the safety of the aircraft may, of course, be referred back to the main base at Baltimore.

By 0600H the control launches and attendant BOAC towing launch are in position at the alighting area and when the aircraft is seen, an aldis lamp signal is sent so that it may more easily locate the alighting area. Voice contact by radio telephone is also established.

During the aircraft's final approach a green lamp signal is given and a green verey light (flare) is fired giving permission to land. If, of course, there is a problem and it is necessary for the aircraft to go around again then a red light and a verey cartridge are substituted for the green signals.

After alighting, the aircraft is led to the selected mooring buoy by the BOAC launch. If necessary, it is towed in.

As soon as the aircraft is on the mooring there is an immediate flurry of activity around it. The first launch alongside is the passenger launch carrying Customs Officer Corcoran or Nugent; a passenger officer; an operations officer; and an engineering officer. The Customs Officer boards the aircraft first and after a brief exchange of information with the Purser, and the receipt of documents from him, authorises unloading to commence. If the Customs Officer is not satisfied with the state of the aircraft, the health aspects, or the flight documents, he may suspend all further activity until he is satisfied.

In the meantime, the operations officer is collecting navigational equipment, codes and cyphers from the Captain and the Navigator and then, as soon as a launch is available, escorts them through the Customs, Health and Immigration controls to the meteorological Office. There the captain will discuss in detail the weather conditions experienced on the flight with the Senior Forecaster on duty. This vital data will be of immerse importance to them for their use over the next day or so. Frequently this was the only source of Atlantic weather data available.

The arrangements for the evening's departure are also confirmed with the Captain—including the amount of discretion to be given to ground staff by the Captain in respect of flight planning and fuel reserve calculations.

Above: Syndey P. Peters, Stan Proud and John Harding, the first Met Office personnel to arrive in Foynes. Right: A group of BOAC staff taken in front of the transit lounge. L-R: Tom Lynch, Jim Barry, Len Studley, Tommy Grant, Tom Liston, Pajoe Carney, Mick Twohig and Bertie O'Connor.

Having been cleared through formalities the passengers are then separated into two groups—one to go to Rineanna and the other to leave from Foynes. Very few are destined to stay in Ireland.

The incoming shuttle flying boat would be met in exactly the same way as the incoming 314 but the crew would remain at the airport while their return load was put aboard. It was unusual for these aircraft to require any fuel or catering as a quick turnaround and an early return to Poole was always required. We did, however always manage to give the crew a real lunch at Boland's Meadow.

Incoming passengers from the land plane shuttle into Rineanna are brought round to Foynes in a leisurely manner to join the passengers who had come across on the flying boat shuttle. A late lunch/high tea would be served at Foynes—either in the terminal or, exceptionally, at Boland's Meadow.

Meantime by about 1500H the forecast for the southbound flight to Lisbon is available and the operations staff complete the flight plan, calculate the essential fuel requirement and tell the ground engineers how much fuel to put into the aircraft's tanks.

At 1600H the Captain is called at the Hotel to wake him and to confirm that he accepts the proposed flight plan and fuel load—and he and the rest of the crew are brought to Foynes, to arrive at approximately 1700H. The flight engineer and cabin staff go straight to the aircraft; the Captain, First Officer, Navigating Officer and Radio Officer go first to the operations room where they get their BOAC briefing, their navigational equipment, codes and cyphers, together with the military recognition challenge and response signals for the duration of the flight. The captain approves—and sometimes amends—the flight plan after he visits the Meteorological office and pays a courtesy call on the Air Traffic Controller. There he would usually be told that his flight plan—lodged in advance by the Operations Room—had been accepted.

This complement of the crew are then taken to the aircraft, in advance of the passengers to check that all is in order, that the flight engineer and cabin staff have done their pre-flight checks, and that the passengers can begin to board. Half an hour before departure one control launch would have done a check of the takeoff area. A BOAC launch would normally have laid a flarepath, even for a pre-sunset departure, since there was always a possibility that the aircraft may return to make an emergency landing after dark.

Once ready and loaded the aircraft control locks are removed; the engines are started, and the aircraft taxies out, usually led by the main control launch and an auxiliary BOAC launch. As soon as the aircraft leaves the mooring area, the buoy would again be made-up in case the aircraft returns before takeoff.

The aircraft's engines are checked thoroughly, in rotation, and then, on a signal from the main control launch the takeoff run would commence. The control launches remain on station for twenty minutes after the aircraft disappears from sight before they return to the quay.

All operational and traffic staff remain on duty for one and a half hours after takeoff before going home. If they went earlier they could not be recalled in time to meet an aircraft which had to return. The flarepath remains in position until it is known that the aircraft is unable to return; because of insufficient fuel remaining in its tanks, or that it had alighted on the water at Lisbon.

The Operations Room itself, remains open, as usual, throughout the day, and does not go off the alert until it is known that the aircraft has safely arrived in Lisbon.

A TYPICAL FEW WEEKS ACTIVITY AT FOYNES AIRPORT

Having examined separately the activities of the three airlines operating through Foynes, perhaps it would be of interest to take a particular period and see what happened from day to day. We have selected the first three weeks of September 1943, during the busy summer period, and set out an extract from the Harbour Register.

As can be seen, there was at least one movement every day and many aircraft spent one and sometimes two nights at anchor at Foynes. The operation of the shuttle can be seen, with Sunderland G-AGHW arriving on Sunday, 5th September, with passengers for Pan Am's Boeing 314 NC18611, returning to Poole with passengers arriving off the Clipper. The level of utilisation is also apparent, with BOAC's Boeing 314 G-AGCB arriving from Lisbon on the 6th and continuing on to Poole only to arrive back at Foynes the same day from Poole on a shuttle flight. The Short S.26 G-AFCI was engaged on shuttle flights from and to Poole throughout the period. Monday, 6th September, was the busiest day, with no less than six arrivals and three departures.

The time taken by the West African services is evident from the transits of Sunderland G-AGHV—arriving in Foynes from Poole on 1st September, continuing on to Lisbon the following day, and then on down to Lagos and back, only arriving at Foynes two weeks later inbound from Lisbon on 14th September, continuing on that day back to Poole.

Arr.	Dept.	Reg. No.	Type	From	To
1st	1st	G-AGEV	Sunderland	Lisbon	Poole
1st	1st	G-AGEW	Sunderland	Lisbon	Poole
1st	2nd	G-AGHV	Sunderland	Poole	Lisbon
3rd	5th	NC41881	VS-44	Botwood	Port Lyautey
4th	5th	NC18611	Boeing 314	Botwood	Botwood
5th	5th	G-AGHW	Sunderland	Poole	Poole
6th	6th	G-AGCB	Boeing 314	Lisbon	Poole
6th	8th	G-AGCB	Boeing 314	Poole	Lisbon
6th	6th	NC18609	Boeing 314	Botwood	Botwood
6th	8th	G-AFCI	Short S.26	Poole	Poole
6th	7th	G-AGEW	Sunderland	Poole	Lisbon
7th	7th	G-AGEV	Sunderland	Poole	Lisbon
8th	13th	G-AFCI	Short S.26	Poole	Poole
8th	8th	NC18611	Boeing 314	Botwood	Botwood
9th	10th	NC41811	VS-44	Botwood	Port Lyautey
10th	10th	G-AGCA	Boeing 314	Botwood	Poole
10th	16th	G-AGHW	Sunderland	Poole	Lisbon
11th	13th	G-AGCA	Boeing 314	Poole	Lisbon
12th	13th	NC41882	VS-44	Botwood	Port Lyautey
12th	13th	G-AGHX	Sunderland	Poole	Lisbon
13th	15th	G-AFCI	Short S.26	Poole	Poole
14th	14th	G-AGHV	Sunderland	Lisbon	Poole
14th	14th	G-AGER	Sunderland	Lisbon	Poole
14th	16th	G-AGHZ	Sunderland	Poole	Lisbon
15th	15th	NC18612	Boeing 314	Botwood	Botwood
15th	17th	NC41881	VS-44	Botwood	Port Lyautey
15th	18th	G-AFCI	Short S.26	Poole	Poole
16th	16th	G-AGEW	Sunderland	Lisbon	Poole
17th	17th	G-AGBZ	Boeing 314	Poole	Lisbon
18th	18th	NC18612	Boeing 314	Botwood	Botwood
18th	20th	G-AFCI	Short S.26	Poole	Poole
18th	20th	G-AGIA	Sunderland	Poole	Lisbon
19th	19th	NC41881	VS-44	Port Lyautey	Botwood
20th	20th	NC18611	Boeing 314	Botwood	Botwood
20th	22nd	G-AFCI	Short S.26	Poole	Poole
20th	20th	G-AGHV	Sunderland	Poole	Lisbon

Pan American Airways, more commonly known as Pan Am, was founded in 1927 by Juan Trippe, and was well know by its famous globe logos and its "Clipper" call sign.

PAN AMERICAN AIRWAYS

It primarily operated as a seaplane service and built up its business buying up smaller airline companies along the coast of the Americas and securing governmental postal delivery contracts, helped with major political backing from the powerful and politically influential backers including William A. Rockefeller and Cornelius Vanderbilt Whitney.

In 1935, Pan Am began commercial flights over the Pacific Ocean from San Francisco to Hong Kong. The Pacific is the world's biggest ocean but it is only a training run in relation to the North Atlantic—the most difficult route in the world.

Pan Am initially used Sikorsky S-40 flying boats, and used a Sikorsky S-42 for their first proving flight from Botwood to Foynes. In 1936 Pan Am asked the Boeing Company to design the first commercial Atlantic aircraft—the Boeing B314.

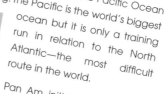

Pan Am had a fleet of six of these long range aircraft, allowing Pan Am to have a regular weekly transatlantic passenger and air mail service over the Atlantic with a single fare costing $375.

The B314 could carry 35 passengers across the Atlantic in ocean liner luxury, indeed, reflecting their "Clipper" call sign based on 19th century clipper ships, the crew of the flying boats wore naval-style uniforms.

B314 FEATURES

A 14 seat dining room serving 7 course meals

Berths and cabins

A tunnel inside the wings to reach the engines

A palatial flight deck for the 7 man crew—captain, first officer, second officer, navigator, engineer, radio officer and junior flight officer

A private honeymoon suite at the rear.

The only bad habit the luxury flying boat had was that if a pilot dipped a wing into the water, gallons of water poured into the dining room when they straightened up.

Today, there are no remaining B314 aircraft. Of the nine Pan Am had, two were sunk, three scrapped, two used for parts, one crashed and one destroyed. Today, the worlds only full size replica is on display at the Foynes Flying Boat Museum.

Imperial Airways was formed in 1924 following the merging of four smaller companies on the advice and encouragement of the government in a bid to establish a single company to strengthen and develop Britain's external air services.

Imperial Airways operated primarily as a land based air service and was the first airline to show a film for passengers en route. In 1927, Imperial Airways developed the Empire Service, serving cities of the empire which included trips that involved train as well as air travel.

Due to lagging behind its European competitors, Imperial Airways merged with British Airways to become BOAC on 1st April 1940, using the Imperial Airways "Speedbird" logo and call sign.

They provided most of the ground services at Foynes—for themselves and for the two American Airlines—Pan Am and American Export.

Nearly all the air traffic across the Atlantic was between America and Britain but during the war, many of these flights terminated at Foynes. Passengers then either took BOAC shuttle flying boats to England or were transferred by bus to Rineanna to go by land plane. Flights from England to Lisbon and West Africa also went through Foynes to avoid the Luftwaffe danger zone around the Bay of Biscay.

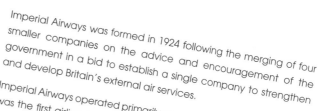

IMPERIAL AIRWAYS

BOAC HAD SEVERAL TYPES OF FLYING BOATS AT FOYNES:

SHORT S.23 C-CLASS
These were the "Empire" flying boats and were mainly used to fly to the cities of the empire.

SHORT S.25 SUNDERLAND
This was the flying boat most often seen at Foynes. It was used for the shuttle between Foynes and Poole harbour.

SHORT S.30 C-CLASS
This was the type of flying boat used for the inflight refueling experiment.

CONSOLIDATED PBY CATALINA
BOAC operated five Catalinas through Foynes. These were used to shuttle passengers from the transatlantic flights to England.

BOAC

Safety -THEN- Comfort!

IMPERIAL AIRWAYS

Helen and Lal Kirwan, BOAC staff, Foynes October 1944

AMERICAN EXPORT AIRLINES

By 1940 Pan Am's monopoly of international air transport was coming to an end. American Export Airlines— founded in April of 1937 and a subsidiary of American Export Shipping—applied for a licence to fly non-stop to Europe in direct competition with Pan Am. Pan Am objected, but the new company was given their licence in July and Captain Charles Blair became their chief pilot.

In 1939 American Export (AEA) placed an order for three Vought-Sikorsky VS-44 flying boat aircraft at a cost of $2,100,000. These aircraft could carry 16 people across the Atlantic non-stop from New York to Foynes.

That same year, AEA made an application to the Civil Aeronautics Board (CAB) for routes across the Atlantic from the United States to the United Kingdom, France and Portugal. On July 15, 1940, and despite protests by Juan Trippe the president of Pan Am, President Roosevelt gave his approval to AEA for a seven-year temporary certificate to serve Lisbon from its base at New York's La Guardia Flying Boat dock. Later services were also flown to Foynes.

AEA could not begin their New York—Foynes flying boat service until June of 1942, due in part to stiff resistance from Pan Am. In 1945 AEA was awarded transatlantic rights covering northern Europe. Following interest from American Airlines, who wanted to break into the overseas market dominated by Pan Am, the CAB approved the acquisition of AEA by American Airlines on July 5th, 1945, and formed American Overseas Airlines (AOA). AEA's name remained until November 1948 when AEA fully merged with rest of AOA's operations.

Top: American Export PBY Catalina "Transatantic", and Above: "Excaibur". Right: Passengers and crew of the "Lieutenant de Vasseau being greeted on arrival at Foynes, 15th July 1938.

Air France's Latécoère 521's arrived in Foynes in 1938 and 1939—the "Lieutenant de Vaisseau Paris" and the "Ville de Saint Pierre". The Latécoère 521 was a 40 ton flying boat. It spanned 162 feet and could carry up to 30 passengers on the Atlantic Route. Routing over Bordeaux, the Latécoère flew up the Bay of Biscay making its landfall at Cork. The purpose of its flight was to look at available airfields in Ireland for a proposed transatlantic flight by a four engined Farman land plane. The crews admired the efficiency of the radio and weather devices at Foynes. However, after September 1939 the war stopped Air France's transatlantic activity.

Air France Transatlantique

BOEING 314

The Boeing 314 "Clipper" was a long-range flying boat produced by Boeing in response to Pan American's request for a flying boat with unprecedented range capability. It is comparable to the British Short Empire. One of the largest aircraft of the time, twelve were built for Pan American World Airways, three of which were sold to BOAC in 1941 before delivery.

The Pan Am B314 NC 18609, 'Pacific Clipper'—which first flew into Foynes on 14th May 1943—made the final Pan Am passenger flight from Foynes to Lisbon on 29th October 1945. Since the start of the survey flights in 1937 Pan Am's Clippers had made a total of 2,097 Atlantic crossings.

Pan Am's Boeing B314 NC18603 'Yankee Clipper' was the first B314 allocated to the Atlantic division and was christened by Mrs. Franklin D Roosevelt on 3rd March 1939. Its first visit to Foynes was on the 11th April 1939 under the command of Captain Harold Gray.

Pan Am's B314 'Atlantic Clipper' NC 18604 first flew through Foynes on 28th August 1939.

Saturday the 18th August 1945 was a record day for Pan American World Airways operations in Foynes, two clippers, the 'Atlantic' and the 'Dixie' arrived from New York in the morning and returned that night. 101 transatlantic passengers were handled at the airport—a record for a day's operation by one airline. Travelling were nationals of Great Britain, Argentina, Sweden, Switzerland, France, Czechoslovakia, Netherlands and the USA.

Top: Pan Am 'Yankee Clipper' moored at Foynes.
Above: BOAC 'Bangor', with the Irish tri-colour in late 1945

Reg.	Type	Name	Service	Status
Boeing 314 operated by Pan Am				
NC18601	314	Honolulu Clipper	1939–45	Sunk by US Navy
NC18602	314	California Clipper	1939–50	Scrapped
NC18603	314	Yankee Clipper	1939–43	Crashed
NC18604	314	Atlantic Clipper	1939–46	Used for parts
NC18605	314	Dixie Clipper	1939–50	Scrapped
NC18606	314	American Clipper	1939–46	Scrapped
NC18609	314A	Pacific Clipper	1941–46	Damaged by storm
NC18611	314A	Anzac Clipper	1941–51	Destroyed
NC18612	314A	Cape Town Clipper	1941–46	Sunk by US Coast Guard
Boeing 314 operated by BOAC				
G-AGBZ	314A	Bristol	1941–48	Sold
G-AGCA	314A	Berwick	1941–48	Sold
G-AGCB	314A	Bangor	1941–48	Sold

SHORT S.30—EMPIRE BOAT

The Short Empire was a passenger and mail carrying flying boat, of the 1930s and 1940s, which flew between Britain and British colonies in Africa, Asia and Australia. It was manufactured by Short Brothers and was the precursor to the more famous Short Sunderland of World War II. In the United States, its contemporary was the Boeing 314.

The origins of the Empire boats lay in an Air Ministry requirement for passenger and mail carriers that could service the colonies particularly to make the connection to Australia. The S.30 series, Cabot, Caribou, Clyde and Connemara, powered by 815 hp Bristol Pegasus engines were fitted with in-flight refuelling equipment and extra fuel tanks so they could be used for a transatlantic airmail service. The idea behind this

SHORT BROS

was for the aircraft to take off and once airborne take on extra fuel to an all up weight of 53,000 pounds giving a range of over 2,500 miles. The extra fuel did reduce the payload to 4,270 pounds against the 6,250 pounds of the standard craft. The refuelling was by three converted Handley Page Harrow bombers, one operating out of Ireland and two out of Newfoundland.

Reg.	Name	Service	Status
Short S.30 operated by Imperial Airways			
G-AFCT	Champion	1938–47	Scrapped
G-AFCU	Cabot	1939–40	To RAF 1939. Destroyed
G-AFCV	Caribou	1939–40	To RAF 1939. Destroyed
G-AFCW	Connemara	1939	Destroyed by fire
G-AFCX	Clyde	1939–41	Damaged by storm, Lisbon
G-AFCY	Captain Cook	1939–53	To TEAL 1940. Scrapped
G-AFCZ	Clare	1941–42	Destroyed by fire
G-AFDA	Ao-Tear-Roa	1939–47	To TEAL 1940. Scrapped
G-AFKZ	Cathay	1941–47	Scrapped

SIKORSKY VS-44

Sikorsky VS-44 were large four-engined USA flying boats built to compete in the transatlantic air travel trade carrying 40 or more passengers across the Atlantic Ocean. Only three were produced, Excalibur, Excambian and Exeter all ordered by American Export Airlines. Sikorsky's standard of luxury boasted full-length beds, dressing rooms, full galley, snack bar, lounge and fully controlled ventilation. During World War II, under a Navy contract the three VS-44's continued flying between New York and Foynes carrying passengers, freight and war material. The first VS-44, Excalibur crashed on takeoff in 1942, ending her life early. After the war, the big Sikorsky 'boats continued to fly for the airline, which had renamed itself American Overseas Airlines (AOA) and was operated by American Airlines.

PBY CATALINA

The PBY was originally designed to be a patrol bomber, an aircraft with a long operational range intended to locate and attack enemy transport ships at sea in order to compromise enemy supply lines. With a mind to a potential conflict in the Pacific Ocean, where troops would require resupply over great distances, the U.S. Navy in the 1930s invested millions of dollars in developing long-range flying boats for this purpose. The Navy adopted several different flying boats, but the PBY was the most widely used and produced.

Although slow and ungainly, PBYs distinguished themselves in World War II as exceptionally reliable. Allied armed forces used them successfully in a wide variety of roles that the aircraft was never intended for. They are remembered by many veterans of the war for their role in rescuing downed airmen, in which they saved the lives of thousands of aircrew shot down over the Pacific Ocean.

PBYs were also used for commercial air travel. Still the longest commercial flights ever made in aviation history were the Qantas flights flown weekly from 29th June 1943 through July, 1945 over the Indian Ocean. To thumb their nose at the Japanese (who controlled the area), Qantas offered non-stop services between Perth and Colombo, a distance of 3,592 nm (5,652 km). As the PBY typically cruises at 110 knots, this took from 28-32 hours and was called the "flight of the double sunrise", since the passengers saw two sunrises during their non-stop journey. The flight was made with radio silence (because of the possibility of Japanese attack) and had a maximum payload of 1,000 lbs or three passengers plus 65 kg of armed forces and diplomatic mail.

LATÉCOÈRE 521

The Latécoère 521 was an outsized flying-boat with strut-braced high wings and short stub sponsons.

The aircraft could transport 72 passengers in a great comfort. On the lower level there was a salon with 20 armchairs and tables, six deluxe double cabins, each with its own bathroom, seating for a further 22 passengers, a kitchen, a bar and a baggage hold. The upper level had seating for 18 passengers, a storage compartment and an office for the three flight engineers.

On the outbreak of World War II the Laté 521 was attached to the French Navy E.6 flotilla, based in Port-Lyautey, Morocco, and was used to patrol the North Atlantic. After the armistice in June 1940 it flew to Berre, near Marseilles, where it was finally wrecked by the retreating Germans in August 1944. The Laté 521 was the basis of the single Laté 522 "Ville de Saint Pierre" civil airliner, and the three Laté 523 navalized variants.

SIKORSKY S-42

The first Pan Am survey flight was completed in a Sikorsky S-42B Flying Boat NC 16736 'Clipper III' under command of Capt. Harold Gray and six crew; N.S. de Lima, W. M. Masland, Walter Smith, H.J. Roberts, C. D. Wright and William Thaler. The meal on board was celery and olive soup, salad, fish, strawberries and cream, iced tea and coffee. After departing Botwood with 2,350 gallons of fuel on board they still had 900 gallons left on arrival at Foynes. The journey was made from Botwood to Foynes in 12hrs. 31mins. The Clipper left Foynes for Southampton, seen off by Col. Charles Lindbergh, who flew to Ireland on 7th July.

The Sikorsky S-42 was an 1930s American commercial flying boat designed and built by Sikorsky to meet a 1931 requirement from Pan American for a long-range transatlantic flying boat. Based on the earlier Sikorsky S-40, the new design provided for an increased lifting capacity to carry enough fuel for a 2,500 mile nonstop flight against a 30 mile-an-hour (48 km/h) wind, at a cruising speed far in excess of the average operating speed of any flying boat at that time. A total of ten S-42s were built. The aircraft first flew on 30 March 1934. The S-42 was also known as the Flying Clipper and the Pan Am Clipper. All Sikorsky S-42s were either scrapped or destroyed in accidents.

SHORT S.23—EMPIRE BOAT

The first series of the Short Empires, the S23, could carry 5 crew, 17 passengers and 4,480 lb (2,035 kg) of cargo at a maximum speed of 174 knots (320 km/h). The range of the S.23 was less than that of the US Sikorsky "Clipper" flying boats and as such they could not provide a trans-Atlantic service. Two boats (Caledonia and Cambria) were lightened and given long range tanks so they could make the trip but that meant they could carry fewer passengers and less cargo.

In an attempt to manage the Atlantic crossing a piggy-back approach was tried. Using a built up S.23 design as the main carrier and a smaller four-engined float plane design, the Short S.20, mounted on its back. Only a single example was built of a carrier aircraft, the S.21 (Maia) and one S.20 (Mercury) together known as the Short Mayo Composite. A successful mid-air launch of Mercury was made in 1938.

MAYO COMPOSITE—SHORTS A20 AND S21

Imperial Airways Mayo Composite composed of a Short S.20 on the back of a Short S.21. This was a most unusual aircraft. On the 19th July 1938 'Mercury' arrived under the command of Captain Donald Bennett. Shortly after the 'Maia' arrived flown by Captain A. S. Wilcockson. The crews were received by Lord Monteagle. The inventor of the 'Piggy Back' aircraft arrived as a passenger on Mercury. Shortly after arrival both aircraft were locked into one. The following day the 'Mayo Composite' left Foynes with the first commercial transatlantic mail load. Directly in front of the pier, on which thousands of people had gathered to watch the two aircraft brake apart—perfectly. It set a new transatlantic record reaching the Newfoundland coast in 13hrs. 29mins. and Montreal in 20hrs. 20mins. and then it continued to New York.

Top: Pan Am Clipper III Sikorsky S-42 arriving in Foyens.
Above: Mayo Composite.
Left: Imperial Airways Short S.23 'Caledonia' being serviced on arrival at Foynes.

AIRCRAFT TO VISIT FOYNES

It is seldom that the opportunity presents itself to list every aircraft to have visited a given airport, but this is possible for Foynes thanks to the comprehensive records maintained by the Harbour Master. The total is 60 aircraft of 13 types:

SHORT

S.23 EMPIRE BOAT

BOAC

G-ADHM	Caledonia
G-ADUV	Cambria
G-AEUD	Cordelia
G-AEUE	Cameronian
VH-ABF	Cooee

S.30 EMPIRE BOAT

BOAC

G-AFCT	Champion
G-AFCU	Cabot
G-AFCV	Caribou
G-AFCX	Clyde
G-AFCY	Awarua
G-AFCZ	Clare
G-AFKZ	Cathay

S.25 SUNDERLAND

BOAC

G-AGER	
G-AGES	
G-AGET	
G-AGEU	
G-AGEV	
G-AGEW	
G-AGHV	
G-AGHW	
G-AGHX	
G-AGHZ	
G-AGIA	
G-AGIB	
G-AGJO	
G-AGLA	(ML 791)

AQUILA AIRWAYS

G-AGKY	Hungerford

S.20

BOAC

G-ADHJ	Mercury

S.21

BOAC

G-ADHK	Maia

S.26

BOAC

G-AFCI	Golden Hind
G-AFCK	Golden Horn

SANDRINGHAM

Antilles Air Boats

VP-LVE	Southern Cross

BOEING 314

314

Pan Am

NC18601	Honolulu Clipper
NC18602	California Clipper
NC18603	Yankee Clipper
NC18604	Atlantic Clipper
NC18605	Dixie Clipper
NC18606	American Clipper
NC18609	Pacific Clipper
NC18611	Anzac Clipper
NC18612	Cape Town Clipper

BOAC

G-AGBZ	Bristol
G-AGCA	Berwick
G-AGCB	Bangor

CONSOLIDATED PBY CATALINA

BOAC

G-AGBJ	Guba
G-AGDA	Catalina 1
G-AGFL	Catalina 2
G-AGFM	Catalina 3
G-AGIE	

American Export

NC18997	Transatlantic

Royal Air Force

FP 202	
UX 330	
UX 422	

LATÉCOÈRE

524

Air France Transatlantique

F-NORD	Lieutenant de Vaisseau Paris
F-ARAP	Ville de Saint Pierre

SIKORSKY

S42

Pan Am

NC16736	Clipper III

VS-44

American Export Airlines

NC41880	Excalibur I
NC41881	
NC41882	

SUPERMARINE

Walrus

Irish Air Corps

N19	
N20	

OPERATORS

OPERTORS

Civil

Air France Transatlantique
American Export Airlines
American International Airways
Antilles Air Boats
Aquila Airways
BOAC
Imperial Airways
Pan American Airways

Military

Irish Air Corps
Royal Air Force

B314

Of all the aircraft that flew the Atlantic at that time the Boeing 314 was the ultimate in luxury. Only 12 Boeing 314's were ever built. Pan Am operated nine and agreed to give BOAC three. Unusually all 12 Boeings transited Foynes before they were divided into an Atlantic and Pacific division. There is none preserved anywhere in the world today unfortunately.

The level of service on the Boeing 314 was of a very high standard. Passengers had a 14-seater dining room with linen tablecloths, crystal glasses and a full waiter service. A typical dinner would comprise of Shrimp Cocktail, Turtle Soup, Steak, Mashed Potatoes, Asparagus, Salad, Peach Melba and petit fours accompanied by a wide choice of drinks. A breakfast menu would be—orange & grapefruit juice, boiled eggs, sliced bananas, preserved figs, dry cereals, fresh strawberries & cream, bacon or Brookfield sausage, rolls,

orange marmalade, currant jelly, hot chocolate, coffee and tea. About 300 lbs of food would be loaded for a transatlantic flight. Two stewards were provided, who prepared all the food for consumption on board. Passengers would find their shoes cleaned and polished overnight. Such a level of comfort was fairly essential however as some of the westbound sectors from Foynes to Botwood stretched to as much as 17 hours. Lavish tipping was then the rule.

Each passenger had a bed to sleep in during the flight.

FLIGHT DECK

The design of the flight deck on a Boeing 314 Clipper broke new ground—it's flight deck took new steps to address the problem of crew fatigue on non-stop ocean flights. The

CREW'S QUARTERS

BAGGAGE

DE LUXE COMPARTMENT

LADIES ROOM

PASSENGER COMPARTMENT

PASSENGER COMPARTMENT

BERTHS

PASSENGER COMPARTMENT

PASSENGER COMPARTMENT

NAVIGATION TURRET

BRIDGE

CATWALK

MEN'S ROOM

Kenneth W. Thompson

solution lay in a commodious flight deck/rest area—a fully carpeted, 9 x 21 foot expanse that not only had walking around room for a 6 to 11 man crew, but quarters for a complete off-duty crew as well. Every flight on a Boeing 314 had a minimum of 11 crew but more often than not it would also have training crew on board. Crew on a Boeing were as follows: 4 Pilots, 2 Engineers, 2 Radio Operators, 1 Navigator and 2 Cabin Attendants.

A cross section of the interior of the Boeing 314 shows at the bow of the plane is the anchor and gear room, which also held a mooring post which would slide out when the hatch was opened. From this room a gangway leads up to the bridge which is entirely lined in black to eliminate glare. Here two pilots handle controls which fly the plane. At the back of the bridge is the navigation and radio room. It is

the directive brain of the ship. Here are (left to right) the radio officer, the flight navigator and flight engineer, all of whom have telephone communication with the bridge. The Captain's office is behind, curtained off. Behind this is the cargo hold, whose main contents would probably be mail. Below, are the galley and dining lounge. Stretched along the length of the ship are seven passenger compartments. The one in the ship's tail is a deluxe compartment corresponding roughly to a ship's bridal suite. At the bottom of the plane, pumps force gasoline stored in sponsons up to the wing tanks and engines. On the plane's very top, shown in cut-through (above) is the celestial observation turret from which the Flying Boat's position is checked by sun and stars.

Lord Headford, station manager BOAC with
Lady Ashley and Douglas Fairbanks Snr.
walking up the street from their flight.

FAMOUS
PASSENGERS
VIPS TRANSITING FOYNES

Passengers in transit to and from America frequently had long stop-overs at Foynes for operational reasons, weather or mechanical delays. For such long transits it was policy to book the passengers into a local hotel, first choice always being the Dunraven Arms at Adare, a delightful village in County Limerick, about 10 miles (16km) from Foynes. One such load of passengers, en route from Foynes to Adare, encountered an unscheduled delay when passing through another village on the way.

Much to the embarrassment of the BOAC traffic officer accompanying the passengers, there was a cattle fair in progress in this village. It took a very long time to get through the narrow village street, crowded with local farmers, each, apparently, with several hundred head of cattle for sale! After that incident, before moving passengers to Adare, there was always a careful check for cattle fairs in progress, with alternative coach routeings planned, if necessary.

A SELECTION OF CELEBRATED VISITORS TO FOYNES 1939–1945

There is a strong hint in the journalist's report in the Daily Telegraph, 5th July 1944 that Winston Churchill, British Prime Minister, travelled through Foynes by flying boat, but this is most unlikely.

In February 1944, actor and decorated naval officer Douglas Fairbanks passed through Foynes followed by Prime Minister of Australia, John Curtin and novelist Ernest Hemingway in May. Also in 1944, Polish Prime Minister Mikolajczjk in June, Czechoslovak Minister Jan Masaryk and New Zealand Prime Minister P. Frazer during July transited through Foynes.

Gracie Fields.

Everyone that was anyone flew through Foynes during those years including from the world of politics, John F. Kennedy, Mrs. Eleanor Roosevelt, Anthony Eden (Foreign and Dominions Secretary), Lord Keynes (Maynard) (Economist, British Treasury), A. P. Herbert (British Minister) and Lord Louis Mountbatten.

Royalty included Prince Ibn Saud (Saudi Arabia), Charlotte, Duchess of Luxembourg, Queen Wilhelmina of Holland, King George of Greece, Olaf Crown Prince of Norway and Prince Bernhard of Holland

People from the world of entertainment included actor and comedian Bob Hope, actors Merle Oberon, Gracie Fields, Bill Rogers, Edward G. Robinson and Humphrey Bogart, and musician Yehudi Menuhin.

(top L-R) John F. Kennedy, Merle Oberon, Yehudi Mehuhin and Mrs. Eleanor Roosevelt.
(bottom L-R) Ernest Hemingway, Humphrey Bogart, Queen Wilhmina of Holland and Bob Hope.

FOYNES

Original IRISH COFFEE

Foynes and Flying Boats will be forever connected with the Irish Coffee as they combined to give us this uniquely Irish treat and, as with anything in Ireland, the weather played a key role.

In 1943, Brendan O'Regan opened a restaurant and coffee shop in the Foynes terminal building. This restaurant had been considered to be one of the best restaurants in Ireland at that time. Chef Joe Sheridan, originally from Castlederg, County Tyrone, had been recruited by Brendan.

Late one night in the winter of 1943 a flight departed Foynes for Botwood, Newfoundland. After flying for several hours in bad weather conditions, the Captain made the decision to return to Foynes and await better conditions. A Morse code message was sent to the control tower at Foynes to inform them of their return. Staff were contacted to return to work and when the flight landed they were brought to the Airport Restaurant for food and drink to warm them.

When Joe was asked to prepare something warm for the passengers, he decided to put some good Irish Whiskey into their coffees. One of the passengers approached the Chef and thanked him for the wonderful coffee. He asked Joe did he use Brazilian Coffee? Joe jokingly answered, "No that was Irish Coffee!!"

A few weeks later, Chef Sheridan knocked on Brendan O'Regan's office door. He showed Brendan this new drink in a stemmed glass and asked him "How about that for eye appeal". Brendan answered "Genius Chef" and so began Irish Coffee. Irish Coffee continued to be served at Foynes to all passengers and is still served to this day to all dignitaries arriving at Shannon Airport.

HOW TO MAKE THE ORIGINAL IRISH COFFEE

1 In your Foynes Irish Coffee Glass, place a teaspoon and fill with boiling water for five seconds.

2 In this pre-warmed glass, put one teaspoon of brown sugar and a good measure of Irish Whiskey.

3 Fill the glass to within 1cm of the brim with really hot, strong black coffee. Stir well to melt all the sugar.

4 Then carefully pour lightly whipped cream over the back of a spoon so that it floats on top of the coffee.

5 Do not stir after adding the cream, as the true flavour is obtained by drinking the hot coffee and Irish Whiskey through the cream.

Sláinte!

Marilyn Monroe enjoying an Irish Coffee

Diane Lynn

Sir John and Lady Mills

Mr and Mrs Kenneth Moore

Brendan O'Regan

Top: Brendan enjoying an Irish Coffee with Stan (Stanton) Delaplane of the San Francisco Chronicle.
Above: The kitchen at Shannon College of Hotel Management founded by Brendan O'Regan.

BRENDAN O'REGAN WAS BORN 15 MAY, 1917, IN SIXMILEBRIDGE, COUNTY CLARE. THE SON OF JAMES O'REGAN AND NORA RYAN, HE ATTENDED SIXMILEBRIDGE NATIONAL SCHOOL BEFORE GOING ON TO BLACKROCK COLLEGE FOR HIS SECONDARY EDUCATION.

James O'Regan, a Chairman of Clare County Council and businessman, would prove to be a major influence on the young Brendan. James was forward thinking, and instilled in his son the belief that the most important thing a person can do is to create work for others—a sense of practical patriotism. When his father purchased the Old Ground Hotel in Ennis, he encouraged his son to follow hotel management as a career. Brendan studied in Germany, France,

Switzerland and Britain and in 1938 returned to manage another one of his father's hotels, The Falls, in Ennistymon, which had associations with Dylan Thomas and Augustus John. However, it also counted senior civil servants as regular guests, and the caterer's energy and verve soon caught their attention. He was asked to manage the St Stephen's Green Club in Dublin, which had been ailing for some time, and successfully turned it into a profitable operation.

In 1943, the Government appointed O'Regan as Catering Comptroller at Foynes flying boat base. The airport had been run by the British up to that point, and O'Regan was conscious of the type of image that the Irish should present to foreign visitors. He employed John and Puetzel Hunt to redecorate the restaurant in order to give it a strong Irish character, and sought well-educated people as restaurant staff in order to give a positive impression of Ireland. He simultaneously maintained good relations with the British to ensure a smooth transition to Irish control.

With the advent of transatlantic land planes at the end of the war in 1945, he was transferred to the airbase at Rineanna (now Shannon) where he continued as Catering Comptroller.

In 1950, O'Regan travelled to the USA as part of a sixteen-man team under the Marshall Aid plan. The visit had a major impact on him, and during his return journey to Ireland by cruise liner he helped to put together a report that would become the blueprint of a vision for Shannon—a vision that was cognitive of social and economic development.

It was also in 1950 that he married Englishwoman Rita Barrow who contributed greatly to his work. They had two sons, Andrew and Declan, and three daughters, Geraldine, Margaret and Carmel.

Brendan went on to be successful in many of his endeavours after leaving Foynes, including developing Shannon International Airport in Rineanna—the successor to Foynes for land planes—and also the setting up of the World's first Duty Free shop at Shannon and the extension of it in the form of the Industrial Free Zone adjacent to the airport.

He established the Hotel and Catering College also in Shannon and lead the restoration of Bunratty Castle and its medieval banquets followed by the restoration of Knappogue and Dunguaire as similar attractions, and the Craggaunowen visitor attraction. In 1961, he founded Shannon Development and later, Obair, a community development organisation centred in Newmarket-on-Fergus.

The outbreak in the late 1960s and the early 1970s of sectarian, political and religious conflict in Northern Ireland impacted on Brendan O'Regan and in 1978, O'Regan founded Co-operation North to overcome violence and unemployment through widespread and ongoing economic, cultural and social co-operation between the Republic of Ireland and Northern Ireland.

Brendan died peacefully, February 2008, having left a permanent mark on the Shannon region, Ireland and the world.

Top: Life long friends Brendan, Bob Dowley (Pan Am Staff and Traffic Manager at Foynes) and Dave Davenport (Pan Am staff and Airport Manager at Foynes) sitting on the harbour wall at Foynes Harbour. Above: Brendan with Museum Patron, Maureen O'Hara Blair at the opening of the Museum in 1989.

Humorous Stories

QUEEN BEES

July 24th, 1944
Senior Representative: Public Relations Officer
Atlantic: Atlantic
Foynes: North Beach

With reference to your recent carriage of three queen bees to Hon. David Gray in Dublin, is it possible to obtain some information about Father Lucey? It would make a snappy story if we could find out whether the reverend gentleman, who is on the instructional staff of one of Eire's leading seminaries, enjoys international fame as a bee-keeper. Also, why was he interested in American bees, especially those from Mississippi?

Incidentally, can you obtain Father Lucey's full name, address, and the title of the post he holds at Maynooth.

(Original signed by J.K. Barnes, Jr.).

PAN AMERICAN AIRWAYS SYSTEM
MEMORANDUM

To: Public Relations Officer, Atlantic Division, North Beach.
Date: August 11th, 1944. From: Senior Representative, Atlantic Division, Foynes.
Ref.: Your memorandum of July 24th, 1944.

In accordance with your request in the reference memorandum, we have obtained some information which should be helpful in the preparation of a story surrounding the carriage of queen bees to the Honourable David Gray for re-shipment to the Rev. Fr. Lucey.

During a recent furlough by the undersigned in Florida, we received a request from Minister Gray to arrange with the Stover Apiaries in Mayhew, Mississippi, to ship three queen bees to New York so that they would arrive about the time the writer would again depart for Foynes. This was accomplished, and the three were subsequently delivered to the Consular group in Foynes who dispatched them by courier car to a pre-determined point between Foynes and Dublin where they were met by a car sent in the opposite direction from Dublin. Shortly thereafter, they were delivered to Father Lucey, and all survived the trip in good form. We might advise here that two previous attempts to deliver bees by the same route were unsuccessful.

Father Cornelius Lucey is a Professor of Logics, Metaphysics, and Ethics at St. Patrick's College, Maynooth. This is an institution which educates the greater number of the Irish priesthood. It is situated about twelve miles from Dublin on the road to Athlone. Father Lucey is a very talented amateur bee-keeper, and sells a good deal of honey, the funds from which are devoted, undoubtedly, to noble purposes. He is a very charming middle-aged man, with a keen sense of fun, and a confidence in bees. He was anxious to get American clipped queens, that is, queens fertilized in America, with the belief that their offspring would introduce new blood into the hive and develop a greater resistance against certain types of disease prevalent here. We have been advised that the queens were accepted by their respective hives and are already at work laying several hundred thousand eggs. The venture is, therefore, 100 per cent successful.

(Original signed by John W. Evans).

c.c. Division Traffic Manager, NBA. Publicity Representative, NBA.

CARRAGEEN MOSS

PAN AMERICAN AIRWAYS SYSTEM
PAN AMERICAN WORLD AIRWAYS
ATLANTIC DIVISION SHANNON AIRPORT, FOYNES

FOR IMMEDIATE RELEASE, MAY 31ST, 1945

Samples of Irish Carrageen Moss are now being flown to New York via Pan American World Airways' Clipper Express service. Prepared in Kerry by Mr. J.J. O'Dowd's organisation at Tralee, these shipments are rushed to American manufacturers for testing purposes in various processes requiring a high grade of Carrageen.

Besides its well-known use in this country as an ingredient for dessert, the New York Times reports issuance of Patent NO. 2,375,259 by the U.S. Patent Office for an unusual new hydrosel - a substance seemingly soluble in a liquid as opposed to a crystallised substance. The product, developed by Gordon Webster Steyle of Wollaston, Massachusetts, is formed of Irish moss (Chondru orispus) known as Carrageen, a marine vegetable growth which is found in limited quantities on rocks nearest the lower limits of the tidal flow around the west and south coasts of Eire. Growing during the spring tide, it is collected by fisher folk during the summer months. Exposure to weather conditions, rain and dew bleaches the Carrageen from a dark shade to a pure white colour. This process has the effect on the Carrageen of removing any substance which may not be in keeping with its uses. Carrageen, when thoroughly white, is then sun dried and stored for dispatch to the market.

The newly-patented process comprises boiling the moss briefly and then

CONTD/

agitating it for thirty minutes to remove the colloid from the gummy resin which binds it structurally in the natural moss. A liquid is obtained of about the consistency of molasses, and laboratory experiments have proved the substance to have wide utility in industrial operations.

It is asserted that the hydrogol will combine readily with liquids as a wetting agent, emulsifier, binder or penetrator. It will hold in suspension chemical solutions.

Mr. O'Dowd, commenting on the future of Irish moss as a valuable export commodity, stated:

For some years past our government had introduced a grading system here for Carrageen Moss, but they have withdrawn this system this year, and to our minds, there is more need this year for the grading of Moss than ever before, owing to the fact that we are trying to get the Irish moss established in the American market, but since the government has withdrawn the grading system, we would like to see the moss properly handled, and marketed according to its grade and we would like to appeal to the gatherers to handle the moss properly, and sell it to the dealers and buyers when perfectly clean and dry, and we would also like to appeal to all the buyers to insist on those conditions when buying the Moss from gatherers. If those rules are carried out fully, I feel certain that there are big things ahead of the Irish Moss trade. With the War now over in Europe, we have to reckon on France being a very keen competitor and our moss export trade instead of falling back into the old rut it was in before the war, will be looked on as one of our brightest export trades, if, as already pointed out, it is properly handled."

Additional shipments of Irish moss will be speeded to the United States via Pan American World Airways this summer.

PAN AMERICAN AIRWAYS SYSTEM

MEMORANDUM

To: Public Relations Officer, Atlantic Division, North Beach.

Date: September 4th, 1944. From: Airport Traffic Manager, Traffic Division, Foynes.

Ref.: PENICILLIN.

On August 21st on Trip 3-267 we received five shipments of Penicillin. We attach a copy of this Manifest for more detailed information. Special arrangements were made in Dublin for the immediate clearance of this valuable drug regardless of documents required and, immediately after arrival; it was forwarded by special car to Limerick, some twenty-six miles distant from Foynes, and there placed on a train which left almost immediately thereafter. It was met in Dublin by a special representative of the consignees.

In today's edition of the "Irish Press", the enclosed article held front page space and, undoubtedly, pertains to the above shipments. We enclose this article in the event you desire to use the information contained therein. Further to the above, you will be interested to know that another shipment of Penicillin consigned to Mr. John O'Sullivan, Dublin, arrived today on Trip 3-277. This shipment has already been dispatched to Dublin in the same manner as above.

(Orig. signed by John W. Evans).

FRUIT FOR A SICK CHILD

PAN AMERICAN AIRWAYS

MEMORANDUM

To: Passenger Service Mgr., Atlantic Div., North beach.

Date: 8 June 1945. From: Senior Representative, Atlantic Div., Foynes.

Subject: Health and Morale Supplies

The personnel at this station certainly appreciate the thoughtfulness of your organisation in placing aboard a recent trip a box containing several cans each of fruit juices and preserved fruits as well as Nestle's cocoa and the other items included. Would it be possible to increase those shipments, perhaps to one a week, and to add some fresh fruit to the contents?

We do not wish to appear demanding because it is realised we have items, such as meat and butter, of which you are extremely short, but fresh fruit is practically unobtainable here. Of whatever quantity received, we would wish to send a portion to the men in London and half a dozen lemons or oranges to the American Minister in Dublin. The latter are forwarded to his friend's small son now recovering from tuberculosis.

(Sgd) Jesse L. Boynton.

The Irish Press

C Do Cum Slóipe Dé asup Onópa na h-Éipeann

The Truth in the News.

Price 1½d.

Mot

Allocations of Penicillin

Commenting on the arrival of American penicillin, an editorial in the current copy of the Journal of the Medical Association states: "We in Ireland not alone owe our American friends a debt of gratitude but also are given the opportunity of utilising our clinical resources for the advancement of knowledge regarding the clinical use of this amazing drug.

PAN AMERICAN AIRWAYS

SHANNON AIRPORT NEWS RELEASE

We feel the following story will be of interest to your readers:

The month of August constituted the busiest period of operation ever experienced by Pan American World Airways at the Shannon Airport in Foynes. Seventeen round trip services from New York were handled, bringing 362 passengers across from America and returning with a total of 860. Of this group, 7 arriving passengers disembarked for various points in Eire and 14 from this country were accommodated to America, mostly on a priority basis. In the field of Cargo more than 4,500 lbs of Clipper Express were flown from New York to Foynes, including some 240 lbs for individual consignees in Eire. The latter shipments consisted of penicillin, bananas, electrical parts and fountain pens. A record weight for penicillin shipments was established when 6,412 lbs were carried out of New York on Pan American Clippers in the month of August, destined to European points. Approximately 30,000 lbs of transatlantic air mail were carried in both directions, including 850 lbs to and from the Dublin Post Office which mail is now forwarded directly to Foynes for carriage.

Released by: R.C. Dowling, Station Manager.

Ref. No. APR/2

Wedding orchids

PAN AMERICAN AIRWAYS SYSTEM

MEMORANDUM

To: Express-Mail Supt., Atlantic Div., North Beach.

Date: 15 June 1945. From: Airport Traffic Manager, Atlantic Div., Foynes.

Subject: Request for shipment by Clipper Express of orchid corsage.

We were today approached with quite an unusual request, but one which we feel might be beneficial to our organisation publicity-wise in Eire.

Mrs. Eamon O'Toole of Limerick requested that we purchase a corsage of four orchids for a girl being married in Limerick on June 27th. Perhaps your office could call a nearby Jackson Heights florist and have him send you the orchid corsage which in turn could be forwarded to Mrs. O'Toole by Clipper Express. This station, of course, guarantees the complete cost of the operation.

We are sure that the Limerick and Dublin papers would give this item complete and beneficial coverage. Please radio the undersigned your acceptance or refusal of this proposal upon receipt of this memorandum.

(Sgd) Elwood R. Alexander.

N.B.: We are enclosing copy of this memorandum for the Public Relations Officer if you are able to make these arrangements and feel that it would be of interest to him.

PAN AMERICAN AIRWAYS SYSTEM

MEMORANDUM

To: Express Mail Supt., Atlantic Div., North Beach.

Date: 28 July 1945. From: Airport Traffic Manager, Atlantic Div., Foynes.

Subject: Clipper Express Orchid Shipment.

Ref: Your WRITE IT of June 19th, Your memo of July 11th

The shipment of orchids in question arrived here in unusually good condition, making the trip over in "I" compartment, which was apparently cold enough to afford ample protection. They were received here in the morning, cleared through Customs and delivered in Limerick to the consignee about three hours later. It proved to be an excellent connection as the wedding was the following morning in Adare, at which time the flowers were as fresh as they would be if purchased in N.Y. then. Naturally considerable comment was caused among those attending the wedding and the bride was extremely pleased with the corsage. Since the time of the wedding, the story has spread considerably as they do in this country.

From a public relations point of view, we benefitted considerably through this shipment. Releases were sent to and printed in Dublin, Cork and Limerick papers, since the story was of natural interest to all of Ireland. As per our radio of July 20th, collection has been effected and is being reported in the customary manner.

(Sgd) Elwood R. Alexander.

c.c. Public Relations Officer, NBA.

PAN AMERICAN AIRWAYS

PAN AMERICAN WORLD AIRWAYS, ATLANTIC DIVISION
LA GUARDIA FIELD, NEW YORK, HAVEMEYER 4-8400

RELEASE ON RECIEPT

Sharing the spotlight with a pretty Irish colleen at a recent wedding in Eire (Ireland) was a corsage of dark purple orchids worn by the dark-haired bride. The flowers were unusual in that they are believed to have been the first flown across the Atlantic especially for a wedding.

A friend of the bride's in Limerick—aware of the fast one-day Clipper Express service from New York to Foynes—called on Pan American World Airways to bring the corsage from the United States for the wedding. The orchids were purchased in Jackson Heights, near PAA's New York base, on a Saturday afternoon, left early Sunday morning by Clipper and arrived early Monday at Foynes, more than 3,000 miles away.

Delivered to the consignee within three hours of arrival, the flowers were worn the next morning by the radiant bride, just as fresh as if they had come from the florist that day. Considerable comment among the wedding guests was echoed by stories in the Eire papers about the unusual corsage.

A pretty Irish bride stepped up to the altar at the Catholic Church in Adare, Co Limerick, on Wednesday, June 27th resplendent in not only the traditional wedding gown but carrying a corsage of dark purple orchids flow specifically from the United Sates. The flowers left New York Monday at 6 a.m. on the Capetown Clipper and arrived early Tuesday morning at Foynes, regular terminus for Clippers flying the North Atlantic.

From Foynes the orchids were sent to Limerick. En route the corsage travelled appropriately in the Clipper's "bridal suite", a large one time lavishly furnished compartment that was converted for cargo at the outbreak of the European war to help relieve the shortage of airplane shipping space. That compartment, located in the tail of the huge flying boat, was kept cool during the trip so that the flowers did not lose their freshness.

County Produce Store at O'Connell Street, Limerick, made arrangements for the corsage through Pan American Foynes office and purchase was made from the Olympia Flower shop, 83-07 Northern Boulevard, Jackson Heights, New York.

Pan American officials stated that it is now possible to make Clipper Express shipments from the United States as they have scheduled a once a week service on non-priority basis.

The contracting parties are:

Timothy McCarthy of Rathcoole, Co. Cork and Mary Condon of Hospital, Co. Limerick

Living in Foynes

FOYNES IS A NEW TOWN BY IRISH STANDARDS, LESS THAN TWO CENTURIES OLD. FOYNES AS A PORT WAS FIRST FORMALLY SURVEYED BY J. F. BURGOYNES, HARRY D. JONES AND RICHARD GRIFFITH. REPORTING TO BOTH HOUSES OF PARLIAMENT AT WESTMINSTER IN 1837 IN THE SECOND ENQUIRY OF THE COMMISSIONERS FOR THE IMPROVEMENT OF THE RIVER SHANNON, THEY PINPOINTED WHAT WAS PROPERLY TO BECOME FOYNES, AND MADE DETAILED RECOMMENDATIONS FOR ITS DEVELOPMENT.

The plans submitted carried an estimated cost of £8,500, and incorporated tidal charts, soundings and other maritime statistics, and so it was that Foynes as a port came into being, and the village development followed naturally.

The terminal building at Foynes Airport 1939-1945 was formally the Monteagle Arms Hotel. It presently houses the Flying Boat Museum and was the headquarters for the Foynes Port Company. Built in the 1860s on lands leased from the Monteagle Estate, it was Foynes' first public bar and hotel, and later the first headquarters for aviation in Ireland. In 1938 when the Department of Transport failed to buy the building, they acquired it by means of a Compulsory Purchase Order.

The village of Foynes had a population of less than 500 people at that time. A large number of personnel moved in to operate the Airport. Foynes had no Hotels, Guesthouses or B&B's. The more senior personnel stayed at the Dunraven Arms Hotel in Adare or in Limerick City. Rates for Hotels varied between 25 and 40 shillings per day including all meals for two adults, but most workers were looking for something locally.

Some rented accommodation in the village. A Nissan Hut converted for accommodation purposes cost 30 shillings a week while wages at that time for passenger services personnel were £3.5 shillings.

Local women decided that renting rooms would provide a good income so they took in paying boarders. After a while the street was lined with HOTEL Signs some of the more unusual were The Crystal Palace Hotel with 4 rooms to rent, or the UNEEDA HOTEL. Surrounding villages also started doing likewise.

Top: Main Street, Foynes with Monument Hill in the background. Pilots used the cross as a landmark. Above: Mr. Ned Scales, Foynes Station Master, 1939.

This proved to be problematic for operations at the Airport. All flights at that time depended on the weather conditions on the North Atlantic. It was not unusual for a flight to depart Foynes or Botwood and fly for five or six hours, hit bad weather and turn back. All communications between the Aircraft and Airport were done by Morse code and Morse code only. All flights departed Foynes late at night for security reasons and arrived early morning.

So for example if a flight left Foynes late at night, flew for five hours, hit bad weather and decided to turn back, they would send a Morse code message to the Tower at Foynes informing them of their decision and their approximate arrival time back at Foynes. The operations man at Foynes then had the problem of contacting staff to come in to work but of course there were no telephones at that time.

To overcome this problem, BOAC, who were not only an Airline operating through Foynes but also operated the Airport facilities, hired a local man and his horse fulltime. The operations man would contact him, give him a list of people he needed to come in to work and where they were staying. The Horseman, Milo, would gallop around the local countryside and call in the workers. This was their answer to a communications problem.

During this period, the port of Foynes functioned as an airport, and a description of its facilities may be of interest. Reference has already been made to the Monteagle Arms Hotel, which had been acquired by the government in 1936 and used to accommodate the met office and radio personnel for the initial trial flights through Foynes.

This now became the Airport Office building and in addition to the met and radio people, it also housed the airport management, the offices of the three operating companies, and the custom service. A building was also provided near to the quayside, where passengers checked in and awaited

Locals watching flying boats arriving at Foynes

their flights. The radio equipment was already in place from the days of the survey flights, as were the mooring buoys. Fuel storage tanks were provided by Shell and ESSO, and launches to bring the fuel out to the flying boats.

Initially aircraft were controlled from a hut on Foynes Island, until a tower was completed on top of the Airport Office Building, which was only brought into use late in 1944. It was a two storey addition to the existing building, the tower at the top being completely glass enclosed, giving a good view of the mooring area, with an airways traffic control room underneath.

Another late development would be the provision of quayside docking facilities but, as will be explained, these were only ready in 1945 and saw little use. Passengers who had to overnight were accommodated in hotels in the locality. The building of a hotel for transit passengers started in 1944.

Like any airport, aircraft took off and landed day and night. Night-time movements must have been particularly spectacular, as the following extract from one of Captain Aidan Quigley's books reveals:

"For a night take off at Foynes, a flare path of lighted guidance buoys had to be laid along the surface of the water. The control launch, with the markers attached to its stern, was always at the ready at the jetty, and when it chugged into the deep waters of the Shannon at dusk to position them, the ten little floats bobbed up and down behind them like ducks in a row.

The direction of the prevailing wind and the best stretch of the river was along the shipping lane, and there the flares were lowered into the water at intervals of 200 yards. As they were laid their lights were switched on—so the drill continued for a mile of the river.

Back at the anchorage near the jetty, the flying boat would be loading up. Last minute adjustments to the engines were carried out from platforms that were hinged down sections of the leading edge of the wing; tools or spare parts that were carelessly dropped fell straight down—into the Shannon.

Now the launch would have positioned itself at the upwind extremity of the takeoff run, but on the inactive side of the flare path. The flying boat lined up at the other end and the sound of its revving engines was accompanied by the aircraft captain's voice coming through the loud speaker in the control launch; 'Ready for takeoff—release Flare Number One'."

The control officer jerked the lanyard of the mortar in the stern of the launch and a parachute flare rocked into the night; its brilliance flooded the whole area with an intense white light. In the distance the powerful propellers of the flying boat was now thrusting masses of spray behind them and labouring its heavy bulk through the clinging surface of the river; finally the waters receded from the bow and the huge craft planed across the Shannon on the step of the hull. Now, on a similar command, the second rocket replaced the dying light of its companion, and moments later the graceful machine was off the estuary and climbing slowly out towards the Atlantic.

The landing preparations were somewhat similar, but after a long ocean crossing, with unpredictable wind and limited navigation aids, the actual arrival time of the big boat could be up to one hour later than the original estimate passed by the radio. This meant a long cold stint for the launch—out at the flare path for an hour and a half before the arrival.

The machine homed into its landing run from radio bearings received from the radio station at Ballygirreen, parachute flares were released as before, and the subsequent touch down was as spectacular as the takeoff. Departures were

Some locals on the main street, Foynes.

generally at night, arrivals at dawn with some daylight operations. Although Foynes was remote from the war zone there was a risk of interception from German long range reconnaissance aircraft during those years—thus the protection of darkness was an added safety precaution.

By April 1944, a fixed flare path had been installed, as well as channel marker lights. Captain Quigley also describes one unusual arrival:

"One arrival at Foynes caused considerable concern to the control staff, the aeroplane did not alight near the flare path and was nowhere to be seen; and although the control officer was certain that it was safely down, the radio bearings indicated its position to be in land.

The flying boat had in fact, been short of fuel, and with bad weather and limited visibility at Foynes the pilot decided not to waste time and alighted on the first suitable water surface that he saw in the area—a tiny creak off the Shannon. The captain taxied the huge machine across to a fisherman and explained his predicament; the man abandoned his own little craft and went aboard the flying boat to guide it home up-river to Foynes."

AIRPORT SERVICES

Airport services and equipment at Foynes were improved; permanent moorings for 8 aircraft were provided and for night operations, 25 flashing channel marker buoys were laid and illuminated flare floats which could be anchored in a line for takeoff or landing guidance were provided.

In 1943 facilities for two aircraft were built, each consisting of a timber pier from shore to the L.W. line and an arrangement of gangways and pontoons to enable passengers to walk to and from the aircraft instead of being ferried by motor launch as before.

Because they availed of BOAC's passenger handling facilities, the Pan Am and American Export presence at Foynes was much smaller than that of BOAC. Each company had a station manager, some administrative personnel and some mechanics. There was a United States Consul based in Foynes to look after the needs of US citizens transiting the port.

Pan Am passengers were accommodated overnight in the Dunraven Arms, Adare, some 16 miles from Foynes, where the crews also stayed. They were taken to and from Adare by BOAC bus. Meals to be taken out of Foynes on the Clippers were handled by a Commissary Representative and were prepared at Foynes.

The report for May 1944 noted that work was still underway on the three aircraft docks and on the control tower. Both the Airport Manager and the Chief Control Officer now appeared in the new uniform specified for airport officials—a dark blue double-breasted uniform with the rank of the wearer indicated by lavender coloured stripes on the sleeve. During the last week of May, BOAC had added to its motor transport fleet a 24 passenger buses, destined primarily for passenger service between Foynes and Rineanna.

In response to a suggestion from head office that company personnel be allowed bring their families to live with them in Foynes, a memorandum was prepared dealing with the housing situation in the area. There was no objection to the proposal—it was pointed out that general living conditions embracing climate, food, clothing and recreation were considered entirely satisfactory and that practically all married members of the BOAC staff at Foynes were accompanied by their families, residing in the quarters at Boland's Meadow or in private accommodation in the town.

It was, however, pointed out that housing facilities in Foynes and its immediate vicinity were severely over-taxed by the employees of the government, operating companies and contractors, and that it was almost impossible to find any housing accommodation. Limited amounts of furniture were available, but at ridiculously high prices.

In March 1945 BOAC reduced the number of personnel going out on the first launch to meet arriving aircraft. Formerly the launch had been cluttered up with mechanics and cargo handlers. The number had now been cut down to the Airport Manager, two station mechanics, one BOAC Passenger Service Representative, two customs officials and one security official.

Efforts to persuade the customs and security officials to meet passengers and crew ashore were unsuccessful. The departure delays were also being brought under control in February, of the seven scheduled departures, four were unable to meet the 2.30pm departure time because of late load arrivals. By March, there was only one delayed departure due to the late arrival of the shuttle load from Croydon.

Main Street, Foynes

Food rationing applied to only three items (tea, sugar and butter) but most foodstuffs were available at controlled prices. Canned foods appeared in limited variety and at great cost. During most of the year, fresh fruits were unobtainable locally, the only substitute being expensive dried fruits and figs. The variety of vegetables was limited and paste foods such as macaroni and spaghetti were not available, as were most sauces, spices and fruit juices.

Practically all items of clothing were available, although not in the same style, quality or low-price range as in America. Soap was rationed in small quantities barely sufficient for personal requirements. "It is impossible to obtain enough soap locally for normal laundering purposes. The laundries themselves have little or no soap and employ cleaning methods which not only fail to clean but, within a relatively

short series of treatments, ruin one's clothing. "Such were the privations of wartime living."

As the report says, "the above points, while inconsequential to residents of hotel or staff quarters, pose major problems to householders and must certainly be considered by personnel attempting to establish independent housing accommodations."

The conclusion was that a company employee, accompanied by his wife, would find it impossible to maintain a private residence in the area at the normal standard of living to which they would be accustomed in America, within the station allowance. The only situation would be for the company to set up staff quarters (as BOAC had done) but this proposal was not pursued.

A new station manager arrived at Foynes in February 1945 and reported his impressions back to head office; "Contrary to an impression obtained in New York, accommodations for staff at Foynes are very comfortable. A few of the staff live in a hotel some distance from the Airport but the majority of the personnel and two of the American Export staff live in a house in Foynes (Ardanoir House) that is operated as a staff house by BOAC.

As a result of fairly recent improvements in food, lighting and heating at this staff house, the personnel are now quite comfortable. The regular shipments of fresh fruit from Lisbon and small packages of such things as Nestle's cocoa from the Commissary Department in New York are proportioned among the staff here and are greatly appreciated by all.

We believe that these add considerably to morale. In spite of recent bad weather which has kept the personnel inside during much of the time available for recreation, the morale

is generally good." A calculation showed that it cost 17/1d per day per employee in Ardanoir House.

Pan Am flight crews were also airing certain grievances about the BOAC facilities at Foynes:

"We have received some bitter, and probably justifiable complaints from crew members about their accommodation at Foynes during their short stay between northbound and southbound flights. If one may judge by the published schedule, our aircraft should arrive at 11.30 and depart at 3.30 local time. Crews would thus have from about 12 noon until 2.30pm, a period of $2\frac{1}{2}$ hours, in which to eat, rest or otherwise divert themselves.

In practice, our aircraft usually arrives between 9 and 10.00am and departs, for reasons discussed above, between 4 and 6.00pm There is still insufficient time available for the worthwhile transport of crews to and from a hotel in Adare or Limerick.

Generally, the crews are provided breakfast upon arrival and luncheon or high tea prior to departure. The interim period of from two to four hours is available for sleeping if they so desire. Aside from the facilities aboard our aircraft, there is only one small Nissen hut, owned and operated by BOAC, for use by all transiting crews.

This Crew Ready Room is normally fitted with chairs, sofas and tables around a small turf stove in the front and larger section; a partition separates this from the rear portion, which has been equipped with six folding cots. Discussions with BOAC have resulted in the following agreement regarding the use and maintenance of this space:

1. The Crew Ready Room will be available for use by our crews from arrival until departure. Supposedly, the crews of other aircraft calling at Foynes during this season will not require this space for any appreciable period.

2. Eleven folding cots and a sufficient number of blankets have been provided.

3. BOAC will assign a full-time attendant to maintain this space. He will keep the fire going throughout the day, air and dry the blankets, when they are not in use, and move most of the furniture to the rear room and prepare the eleven beds in the main heated room on the days of our aircraft arrivals.

We realize fully that these accommodations for the crews during their short lay-over here leave much to be desired insofar as comfort is concerned. However, we shall be unable to arrive at a more satisfactory arrangement without a very considerable outlay of money for equipment and space."

Above Left: Bernard Madigan (BOAC messenger boy), with a Boeing 314 navigator, Suthcliffe.
Above Right: Mr. Grogan, working in the electricity generation station at Fopynes. Electricity was generated at the time using a water turbine system from the local sawmills.

INTELLIGENCE AT FOYNES.

Ireland was a neutral country during the second world war. In 1940 the Irish Government imposed a news blackout on Foynes. No journalists, cameras etc. were allowed into Foynes. Locals only found out about VIP's passing through long after they had departed.

Captain Stapleton was a member of the Irish Air Corps. As civilian air travel was just being established in Ireland, Captain Stapleton was appointed as Head of Air Traffic Control at Foynes.

On being assigned to Foynes, an Irish Army Intelligence Officer was presented with a round of duties, sometimes to board a plane to inspect the interior, in the absence of another officer. Otherwise, to meet passengers on the pier, to prevent them encountering unauthorised persons, examine passengers with the help of an army sergeant, to observe all visitors while in Foynes and, if possible, to converse with passengers.

'At embarkation collect as much information about each passenger as possible without giving an impression of third degree. If a group appears interesting, ask them each different questions and collate the various answers...keep your ear to the ground all the time and for everything.'

All passenger manifests had to be submitted in advance of flights, many travelled under false names and passports. In 1939 and 1940 all military personnel had to travel through Foynes in civilian clothing but this rule was gradually relaxed. Those who worked in Foynes at that time say the joke going around was "Who are we neutral against?"

What most people do not realise is that Foynes became a vital escape route for refugees from the war in Europe. If they could get on a flight in neutral Lisbon they would be flown into Foynes and await a seat on a flight to America to begin a new life. Over the past number of years many of these former refugees have returned to Foynes and told us their stories.

PERSONNEL PASSING THOUGH FOYNES

In May 1943 numbers of distinguished army officers passed through probably because 'of the preparations for the talks at Casablanca'. U.S. passports issued to members of 'combat forces' were marked 'civil servant'. RAF personnel and British Army personnel were described, respectively, as Air Ministry and War Office officials. During the period from September 1942 to December 1943, 1,009 U.S. Army personnel, 1,057 U.S. Navy personnel, 409 British War Office personnel, 909 British Air Ministry personnel, 300 British Admiralty and 854 Refugees and Repatriates passed through Foynes.

INTELLIGENCE REPORT, FOYNES, SEPTEMBER 1944

Passengers U.S.A. to U.K. and beyond.

Stanislaw Fischlowitz	Polish Minister of Labour
Ludwik Grosfeld	Polish Minister of Finance
Lord Keynes	British Treasury
Sir David Meek and Staff	Dept. of High Comm'er for India
Hendrik L. H. Kauffman	Danish Minister in Washington
Bishop Andrew Yu-Yue Tau	Visiting Archbishop of Canterbury
Ling Chieh Kung	Envoy/E Min Plen. Nephew Mde.
	Chiang-Kai-Shek
Pierre Krier	Lux'berg Min. for Social Affairs
Carl Hambro	Pres. Norge Storthing (later returned UB)
Georges Theunis & wife	Former Belg. Prime Minister
Yehudi Menuhin	Famous Violinist
Sir. Geo Campbell	Brit. High Comm'er in Canada
Walter Horgan	U.S. Representative for State of Washington
Chester Holefield	U.S. Representative for State of California
J. P. Richards	U.S. Representative for State of S. Carolina
Karl Earl Mundt	U.S. Representative for State of S. Dakota
W. H. Judd	U.S. Representative for State of Minnesota
Brooks Hays	U.S. Representative for State of Arkansas
Wm. Poage	U.S. Representative for State of Texas
Clark Fisher	U.S. Representative for State of Texas

U.K. and beyond to U.S.

F. Vondtich	Po I. Consultants to Relief Committee
E. Lobl	Po I. Consultants to Relief Committee
Dr. Wellington Koo & Staff	Chinese Ambassador to U.S.A.
Karl Evang	Norg. Dir. General for Public Health
Harold Butler	Dir. General Brit. Information Services
Ernest G. Robinson	Film Actor
Nicolai Feoney	Russian UNRRA Representative
Ivan Illuischenzko	Special Mission to U.S.A.
V. Soloviev	(Probably Military) from Moscow.

Embarking Passengers

There appears to now be space available westbound, and "ordinary passengers" are sometimes carried. These are mostly U.S. Citizens returning, Irish girls who have married U.S. Nationals who were stationed to the North of Ireland or Irish State Officials.

Top: Captain Ned Stapleton, Head of Air Traffic Control at Foynes. Above: An intelligence report, illustrating the breth of the passenegers and their nationalities that transitted through foynes.

Foynes Photo Album

THE END OF AN ERA

BETWEEN 1941 AND 1945 APPROXIMATELY 48,000 PASSENGERS PASSED THROUGH FOYNES. BETWEEN 1941 AND 1943 FOYNES HAD ABOUT 2,080 JOURNEYS BY FLYING BOATS. BETWEEN 1939 AND 1943, 150,876LBS OF MAIL WERE LOADED ONTO FLYING BOATS AND 197,318LBS OF MAIL OFF-LOADED AT FOYNES.

Hostilities in Europe ended in May 1942, although World War II did not officially end until September 2nd 1945, government priority on all commercial travel continued until it was lifted on October 15th 1945. Nevertheless from June 1945 onwards there was a gradual increase in the number of civilians, mostly businessmen, using the Flying boat services through Foynes.

When the Pan American "Atlantic Clipper" arrived in Foynes on 11th August 1945 with 34 passengers and 939lbs of mail and 625lbs of Clipper Express Cargo, this was the greatest number of passengers ever carried across the North Atlantic at that time. However by that stage the days of the Flying boats were numbered. The war had given new impetus to the development of a number of airfields on both sides of the Atlantic. The land plane had also reached a stage of development where it was now much more efficient and capable then the Flying Boat and available in much larger numbers, all of which spelled the end of the Flying boat era.

On Monday 22nd October 1945 the final American Export departure took place under the command of Captain Charles Blair. Hundreds of people gathered at Foynes to watch the departure for Botwood. Captain Blair took off at 6.30pm with 16 passengers and made a low pass over Foynes and Limerick by way of final tribute before heading out over the Atlantic.

From 1937 to the end of scheduled services Foynes had played a pivotal role in first developing and then maintaining transatlantic air services—a role which has ensured its place in history. By 1946 the day of the Flying Boat had passed but at least the hectic aviation activity which Foynes had witnessed over the years was not leaving the area, merely moving a few miles by river to Rineanna.

CHARTER FLIGHTS:

Even though scheduled services had stopped using Foynes many charter flights operated up to 1949.

One unusual Charter flight operated by American International Airways through Foynes on October 13th 1947—the Bermuda Sky Queen—formerly the Pan Am Boeing 314, Capetown Clipper. It had on board 61 passengers—the greatest number of passengers ever flown across the Atlantic in a Flying Boat. However watching the takeoff locals and officials at Foynes were greatly concerned as it took for ever to get off the water and many were concerned that it would never make it to Botwood. They were right. The Bermuda Sky Queen was forced to come down in mid-Atlantic after running out of fuel.

The 42 ton Flying Boat had not taken into account the full force of the Atlantic head-winds. In addition the plane's load was 5,000lbs over her maximum weight—the equivalent of 25 people plus their baggage. The US Coast Guard cutter George M Bibb came to their rescue and not a single life was lost after a 48 hour rescue operation. Before leaving the scene the Bibb shelled the flying boat so that it would not be a danger to navigation. The US Civil Aviation Board held an investigation into the affair. The Charter company was closed down and the owners charged with engaging in foreign transport of passengers without authorisation.

On October 11th 1949 Aquila Airways Short Sunderland 'Hungerford' arrived at Foynes on it's way to Lisbon. It left Foynes with 50 passengers, 12 English and Scottish and 38 Irish for a pilgrimage to Fatima. Aquila Airways was one of the more interesting British Independent airlines of the post war period. The 'Hungerford' was to be the last passenger flight through Foynes

The 'Hungerford' was damaged in a take off accident at Southampton on 28th January 1953 and was subsequently scrapped. Aquila Airways ceased operations in September 1958.

Top: Aquila Airways Short s.25 leaving Foynes for Lisbon.
Above: Passengers and crew of the Bermuda Sky Queen being rescused mid-Atlantic.

A journey back to Foynes

MAUREEN O'HARA-BLAIR
PATRON OF THE FOYNES FLYING BOAT MUSEUM

"I WAS THERE THE EVENING HE SAID GOODBYE," SAID HARRY CRIPPS, ONE TIME TRAFFIC WARDEN FOR PAN AM IN LONDON. "CHARLIE BLAIR ROARED OFF THE WATER, CIRCLED THE TOWN, AND THEN FLEW DOWN THE LENGTH OF THE MAIN STREET IN A FAREWELL SALUTE.

The people of Foynes, with tears in their eyes watched him ride the west wings of the Atlantic, higher and higher, until they could see him no more, then they went to bed and closed their doors on their broken hearts. It was the end of an era, the end of the great and glamorous days for Foynes.

Foynes closed as an air terminal on October 22nd, 1945, and Captain Charles Blair, of American Export Airlines, piloted the last flying boat, a Sikorsky VS44, to leave the port. He arrived in New York October 23rd. The next day he turned around and flew the first scheduled transatlantic land plane to Shannon Airport on the other side of the river from the bereaved Foynes.

Foynes had been the biggest, most prominent, international air terminal in the world. It was there that all the transatlantic airline proving flights to New York originated in 1936. The famous flying boat pilot Captain J.C. Kelly-Rogers was one of the early captains on those proving flights.

Sir Alan Cobham, ran his inflight refueling company out of Foynes in the 1930's, carrying mail to the U.S.A. He designed the first significant transocean air refueling technique for flying boats.

American Export Airlines, Pan American Airways, and British Overseas Airways Corporation, the only airlines flying the Atlantic in those days, used Foynes as their international base.

Flying boats, filled with military "highbrass", in civilian clothes, and high ranking government officials, who were pursuing the war effect, flew in and out of Foynes, back and forth between Britain and the U.S.A. Foynes was a hustling, bustling, important port.

Then, as Charlie Blair described it, after World War II, " They paved the world with concrete, land planes took over the air routes and the great, and romantic flying boat bases were closed."

Foynes became a quite village, but the old people never tired of talking about the great days. Their children, and then their grandchildren, didn't always listen. Then, out of the mist of yesterday, their hero came back to give truth to the stories.

It all started, I am sure, the very day Charlie Blair left Foynes, but during Easter 1975, when we were in Ireland for a few days, we drove to Foynes, so he could take a look at the old base. He walked down by the water, and found the disembarking ramp still there, a little weary, a little tired, but still floating on the Shannon tide.

Three curious men watched him in the cold, dockside breeze. They asked what he was looking for and could they be of any help. Charlie asked them if the old flying boat mooring was still in the water.

The older man raised his head and took a long look at Charlie.

"Why do you want to know?" he asked.

"Well," I answered, "he is thinking of landing a flying boat out there this summer like he used to many years ago."

There was a glint in the men's eyes. The glint blossomed into an unbelieving glow of sheer delight. An arm came up, and a finger pointed straight at Charlie.

"You're not Captain Charlie Blair!" one of them said.

He squinted his eyes. "You are Captain Charlie Blair!" In a rush of words he continued, "I used to work on the boats that ferried the passengers back and forth to your flying boats." Hands clasped hands, and pumped them up and down, in pleasure and in disbelief, and I'm sure that night the whole village knew Captain Charlie Blair was coming back in the summer.

On July 6th, 1976, the Antilles Airboats' four engined Sandringham flying boat, Southern Cross took off from Chrisiansted Harbour, to begin the long, sentimental flight to Foynes, Ireland, via Boston and Gander Lake, Newfoundland. Charlie was at the controls. On board were five crew, three guests, and ten family members of the crew, including seven children. Five more guests boarded in Boston.

On July 8th, 1976, Charlie Blair's old friends at Shannon Airport Control Tower were listening, waiting and watching for him to arrive at 11.15am, Irish time. At 11:04am, he broke through the clouds over Foynes, crossed the river and flew over Shannon Airport to say "hello". He made two circles over Foynes, then gently touched down on the welcoming waters of the estuary—31 years after he had left.

Sitting on the lower deck I wondered how Charlie felt, and if there wasn't a glisten in his eye behind the dark glasses. I know I felt a lump in my throat the minute the great flying boat touched the water.

Then we looked at the shore. Thousands of people lined the dockside and the old slipways. We had not expected such a welcome. Bagpipes were playing, people were waving and shouting: "Welcome Back". Irish, English, and world press representatives were there and the T.V. cameras were rolling.

The Commodore of the Foynes Yacht Club, Dan O'Sullivan had graciously arranged for us to be ferried ashore and had arranged a huge reception for us at the Yacht Club.

We learned that they had even closed the schools for the day, so the children could see for themselves what it must have been like in those golden days of aviation.

As we made slow progress through the throngs of wellwishers, I could not help but notice how many old people were there, mostly men, some bent over heavy sticks, who wanted to shake Charlie's hand and smile gently at him. Some just touched him and some stood and looked, their eyes filled gently with yesterdays and unspoken "thank you's" to their hero for coming back. I was deeply touched.

At the Yacht Club, more surprises awaited: Captain Ned Stapleton, who was Chief Traffic Control Officer during all the flying boat years at Foynes; Thomas Crawford Young, who refueled the first flying boat to cross the Atlantic in 1937; Captain Roly Alderson, from B.O.A.C., who 53 years ago, flew the three American built B-314 flying boats, Berwick, Bangor, and Bristol, into Foynes on the delivery flight to Britain from the Boeing factory; Captain John Grierson, famous British wartime pilot and author; Brendan O'Regan, chairman of the Shannon Development Company, who had been controller of the catering services at Foynes; Charlie McCarthy, who had been Pan Am Chief; Con McGovern, retired Pan Am manager in Dublin who, as a young Irish Army Lieutenant, was on security duty at Foynes when Captain Blair landed there in 1942; Pat Ryan, chairman of the Limerick County Council; J. Barrett, chairman of the Foynes Harbour Trustees; Tom Morris, Chairman of the Limerick Chamber of Commerce and many other old friends.

> **"THOUSANDS OF PEOPLE LINED THE DOCKSIDE AND THE OLD SLIPWAYS. WE HAD NOT EXPECTED SUCH A WELCOME"**

The din was deafening. There were speeches, and toasts, happy voices, laughter and tears of sentiment. Brendan O'Regan presented to the Foynes Yacht Club the famous sculptured head of Mannanan Mac Lir, the Irish God of Sea and Wind, in Charlie's name. It was placed permanently infront of the clubhouse, faced forever into the wind and sea, with the dedication: "Captain Charlie Blair, the last to leave, the first to return."

Maureen O'Hara Blair

Top: Captain Charles Blair with Maureen O'Hara in the cockpit of a 747.
Left: Captain Charles Blair greeting Captain Jack Kelly Rogers at Killaloe in 1976

FOYNES FLYING BOAT MUSEUM

The Foynes Flying Boat Museum, housed in the original terminal building in Foynes, recalls that nostalgic era when Foynes became the centre of the aviation world from 1937 to 1945. On July 9th 1939, Pan Am's luxury Flying Boat, the "Yankee Clipper" landed at Foynes to become the first commercial passenger flight on a direct route from the USA to Europe. During the late 1930s and early 1940s, this quiet little town on the Shannon became the focal point for air traffic on the North Atlantic. Now the "Yankee Clipper is back—our latest exhibit is the world's only full scale replica of the Boeing 314, "Yankee Clipper". You can travel back in time and see for yourself what it was like to be a passenger in one of these wonderful flying boats.

In 2001 after many years of effort, with financial support from the Department for Arts Sport & Tourism, we purchased the entire Terminal Building from Shannon Foynes Port Company. This was a dream come true. The building comprises 37,000sq feet of space and will shortly be listed as a protected structure.

Some years ago the Museum board drew up a development plan for further expansion at the Museum over a number of years so that we could put on display the vast amount of memorabilia and artefacts that have been donated to us since opening.

Having made representations to the former Minister for Arts Sport & Tourism, John O'Donoghue T.D. in 2005 we were

We also have a comprehensive range of exhibits and graphic illustrations. You can learn about the history of the flying boats in our authentic 1940's cinema, featuring the award winning film 'Atlantic Conquest'. We showcase the original Terminal Building, Radio and Weather Room, complete with transmitters, receivers and Morse code equipment. The exhibits feature an introduction to the first transatlantic passenger service and Foynes during the war years.

The Flying Boat Museum was established in 1989 in part of the original airport terminal building at a cost of £450,000. It has expanded enormously over the years and today the Museum Company own the entire Terminal Building. It is open yearly from March 1st to December 1st Maureen O'Hara Blair officially opened it on the 8th July 1939 and she continues to be it's Patron.

Most aviation museums deal specifically with military aircraft while we tell the story of the development of passenger travel and Ireland's vital role in that development. We also honour the pioneering men and women who worked in Foynes or passed through it.

delighted when he fully endorsed our plans and announced a grant of €1.5 million for our expansion programme.

Under the expert guidance of our Historical Interpreter, Jack Harrison, we expanded the museum with further exhibition rooms and one particular area for children that includes three flight simulators allowing visitors to try their hand at flying these big heavy Boeing B314 Flying boats. This also allowed us to cater for much larger groups and also gave us a function room/concert hall.

However the jewel in the crown was the building of a full scale replica of the Boeing B314 Flying Boat. A contract was signed with Bill Fallover, a film set builder based in County Wicklow to build us a full scale Boeing B314 flying boat—this would be the only one in the world as none were ever preserved.

Bill did a truly wonderful job and today this is the big attraction at our Museum. Visitors can walk through it, see the sheer size, look into the honeymoon suite and climb upstairs to the cockpit and experience the luxury of travelling at that time.